The Nature of
Information Technology
Managerial Work

The Nature of Information Technology Managerial Work

The Work Life of Five Chief Information Officers

CHARLOTTE S. STEPHENS

QUORUM BOOKS
Westport, Connecticut • London

Library of Congress Cataloging-in-Publication Data

Stephens, Charlotte S.
    The nature of information technology managerial work : the work
life of five chief information officers / Charlotte S. Stephens.
       p.   cm.
    Includes bibliographical references and index.
    ISBN 0-89930-920-8
    1. Information technology—Management—Case studies. 2. Chief
information officers—United States—Case studies. I. Title.
HD30.2.S783   1995
658.4'038—dc20   95-809

British Library Cataloguing in Publication Data is available.

Library of Congress Catalog Card Number: 95-809
ISBN: 0-89930-920-8

First published in 1995

Quorum Books, 88 Post Road West, Westport, CT 06881
An imprint of Greenwood Publishing Group, Inc.

Printed in the United States of America

The paper used in this book complies with the
Permanent Paper Standard issued by the National
Information Standards Organization (Z39.48–1984).

10 9 8 7 6 5 4 3 2 1

Copyright Acknowledgment

The author and the publisher gratefully acknowledge permission to use the following:

Reprinted by permission of *Harvard Business Review.* An excerpt from "The Manager's Job: Folklore and Fact," by Henry Mintzberg (March/April 1990). Copyright © 1990 by the President and
Fellows of Harvard College; all rights reserved.

Contents

Appendices

Tables

1

The Chief Information Officer: Why?

INTRODUCTION

In the 1980s, the top information systems (IS) manager's job grew in rank and importance. In fact, a new executive role emerged and the emergence of this role bespeaks an even greater change. Although the role is called Chief Information Officer (CIO), the title is usually Senior Vice President, Executive Vice President, or Vice President. Seventy-three percent of the *Fortune* 100's top IS managers have titles of Vice President or above (Brumm 1988b, 90). Furthermore, these top Information Systems managers are within two levels of the CEO. Whereas in 1988 80% of the top IS managers reported within two levels of the CEO, only 44% did in 1968 (Davis 1974, 374). In 1988, 27% reported directly to the CEO, but only 12% did in 1968. A significant change has occurred.

The title, "Chief Information Officer" or CIO, was first used by Synnott and Gruber in 1981. They defined the CIO as "the senior executive responsible for establishing corporate information policy, standards, and management control over all corporate information resources" (Synnott and Gruber 1981, 66). More than a decade later, the term, if not the title, has become commonplace. Over 700 articles have used this term in the past five years, according to *Abstracted Business Index*'s database. Why did this new role emerge? Why is the CIO's work so important?

Studying articles, books, and unpublished doctoral dissertations and spending 215 hours observing five successful CIOs has led to four answers to these questions:

1. Survival
2. Competitive advantage
3. Restructuring
4. A new paradigm.

But why ask why? These reasons have important implications for organizational success in the 1990s. The CIO is part of what Alvin Toffler has called a wave of change. The CIO is a leading indicant of whether an organization participates in this change.

WHY IS THE CIO'S WORK IMPORTANT?

Survival

Survival, in a word, is the reason why the CIO's work is important. The organization's survival may depend on the CIO's ability to bridge the gap between information technology and the firm's strategic objectives. According to John Donovan, professor of management at MIT and chair of the Cambridge Technology Group,

If they [information managers] don't move to the strategic end, they will be lost. And so will the companies they serve. I am talking about survival. . . . Even our economic power base is at risk. History shows that wherever economic power goes, ideologic power follows. What happens if economic power shifts from the U.S. to Japan?

Every one of us must understand what is at stake, what we could lose if the gap is not closed between MIS executives and the strategic objectives of the firm. (Donovan 1989, 84)

The CIO must close the gap between the use of information resources and the strategic objectives of the firm. Integrating information technology and corporate strategy is a matter of survival in an intensely competitive global economy.

Competitive Advantage

A second answer to the question of importance is competitive advantage. Beyond survival, the CIO must enable the firm to deploy information technology to prevail, to gain a competitive advantage. Largely based on Michael Porter's (1985) work on the competitive forces (new entrants, buyers, suppliers, substitutes, rivals), a body of literature has been generated on the use of information technology to gain competitive advantage. Two cases are invariably cited: American Hospital Supply's placement of terminals in hospitals and American Airlines' placement of terminals in travel agencies.

American Hospital Supply

American Hospital Supply originally placed the terminals in hospitals as a cost-cutting strategy, off loading the entry of orders to the customer. A surprising by-product of this new customer capability was that the American Hospital Supply system could be used by customers to check on the status of orders and to reduce their own inventory since orders could be filled more quickly. The time involved in completing the paper form at the hospital, forwarding the paper form to American Hospital Supply, and then entering the form at American Hospital Supply was compressed. As a result, costs were reduced for both customer and supplier and the supplier's market share was increased. The unanticipated result was that the supplier's market share was increased; the system provided a competitive advantage.

American Airlines

American Airlines first placed terminals in travel agencies to automate reservations. Other airlines who wanted to make information available to travel agencies could use the American Airlines SABRE system, but American always listed its flights first. As a result, American increased ticket sales and created a window of opportunity for the firm even though other airlines responded with their own systems.

Other Examples

Howard Anderson, Managing Director of the Yankee Group, cites Otis Elevator's use of information technology to decrease the threat of substitute service. Otis found that

service was becoming a commodity. If Otis would repair your elevator at $40 an hour, someone else would come in and repair it at $36 an hour. Otis put chips into each of those elevators and . . . started remotely monitoring. Now, the Otis repairman would come by and the building manager would ask why he was there since the elevator wasn't broken. And the repairman would reply: it's just about to but I can fix it before it does. (Anderson 1989, 42)

Otis also analyzed its market and found that

a relatively small number of architects design skyscrapers, massive hotels, that sort of thing. And very cleverly what Otis did was build a communications link between itself and these architects. . . . Otis put a PC terminal on the architect's desk. The architect found all he had to do was work off of a data base, and the elevator could be designed in a third of the time. For the architect, great labor savings. For Otis, Market share went up 8 percent. (Anderson 1989, 42)

Using information technology for competitive advantage is one of the most popular topics in business literature today. In a survey sponsored by Arthur Andersen & Company, CEOs were "nearly unanimous in believing that information technology could give their firms competitive advantage" (Brown et al. 1988, 26)

The CEO's Relationship with Information Technology

However, this survey also "clearly indicates that very few CEOs know how to accomplish this objective." Despite the fact that "IS [Information Systems] now touches every business activity of a company offering a product or service—from conceptualization, design, and production, to marketing, distribution and support" (Perry 1986, 38) few CEOs are familiar with information technology. According to a First Market Research, Inc. telephone survey of 103 *Fortune* 1000 CEOs in February and March of 1989, 58% of CEOs do not use a computer at all and of that 58%, 64% do not plan to use a computer in the future.

Peter Keen (Rifkin 1989) provides three categories for CEOs and their relationship with information technology:

- Those who wish technology would go away
- Those who think the job should be upgraded and delegated to a "heavyweight" in the organization and who just want someone to "take charge and keep it away from me"
- Those who see IS as a part of everyday life and recognize that the IS chief now must be part of top management.

Keen says that only about 20% are in the last category. Nevertheless, the CIO is the corporate executive who enables the firm to deploy information technology for competitive advantage.

Restructuring

Keen believes the focus of information technology should be inward, toward restructuring the organization. Michael E. Treacy, of MIT's Sloan School of Management, likewise believes that the use of information technology for competitive advantage needs to be reconsidered. He "fears many industries may cripple themselves. He cites the effects of computerized reservation systems on airlines: 'customers have a better bargaining position and prices have been eroding" (Harris 1985, 114). Internally, the CIO must be a key player in the critical transformation of large, centralized, hierarchical organizations to large, decentralized, "flat" organizations. Restructuring, then, is a third answer to the question of importance.

Span of Communication

Peter Drucker's (1988) much heralded information-based organization with a span of communication rather than span of control will depend on a technology infrastructure to manage the information flow throughout the organization. Donovan has even suggested that a more appropriate title for the CIO is Network Manager. Keen calls this internal strategic objective the creation of a new organizational architecture made possible by information technology:

Large organizations—both in industry and government--are reaching the limits of complexity. . . . Complex organizational structures are now impeding the missions of organizations. Information technology planning should therefore focus on simplifying organizations, to ensure their health. Chief executive officers should look to information technology to help them design their organizations.

Organizations can be simplified by increasing direct contact between people. . . . Information technology can help by reducing the need for intermediaries, thereby flattening organizational hierarchies. The technology also can help organize information for easier access . . . Management should shift its attention from the use of information technology for competitive purposes to using it to redesign their organizations to operate more simply. (Keen 1987, 1-3)

The CIO's strategic role of "linking IS to the business" (Benjamin et al. 1985) means linking IS to the business internally and externally. The CIO is charged with interfacing the organization with its environment to gain competitive advantage and interfacing the work units within the organization as large, complex, geographically dispersed organizations seek flexibility in a rapidly changing environment.

A New Paradigm

A fourth answer to the question, "Why is the CIO's work important?" is that the CIO represents a new paradigm for information systems and information resource management. The CIO must lead the information resource group through major changes in their function and focus. Joel Barker (1985) has defined a paradigm as a "set of rules and regulations that (1) describes boundaries and (2) tells you what to do to be successful within those boundaries. A paradigm shift occurs when the 'rules' change, thereby changing the means of being successful" (McNurith,1988b, 13).

According to Barker, perceiving paradigm shifts creates windows of opportunity and reduces the future shock of change, thus lowering resistance to change. Anytime a person changes roles, a paradigm shift occurs. The strategic role played by a CIO is such a paradigm shift: The set of rules and regulations which describe the information executive's boundaries and what is required to be successful has changed. This leading IS role provides the paradigm for the information systems manager and employee.

An Imperative for Change

The fundamental shift for IS managers and employees is that they can no longer separate themselves from the business in which they work and are effective: "They can no longer see themselves as just data processing specialists who happen to be applying their trade at an insurance company, bank or airline. . . . The MIS function is in the midst of its most significant restructuring since the role began evolving more than 30 years ago. And all bets are on the changes accelerating and becoming even more complex rather than subsiding into a new clearly defined structure"(Kirkley 1988, 79).

According to R. Talmadge Fish, manager of information systems at Burlington Industries, Inc., "The information systems function will not exist as it's presently constituted" (Kirkley 1988, 79). Just as technology, particularly telecommunications and microcomputers, is changing the organization's structure and enabling it to respond more quickly, technology such as application development tools and Computer-Assisted Software Engineering (CASE) are changing the IS organization and enabling it to respond more quickly.

According to Michael Scott Morton, professor at MIT's Sloan School of Management, "If there's one imperative now for IS, it's the crucial management of change" (Kolodziej 1989, 73). A similar conclusion was reached by Patricia LaRosa, a doctoral candidate at Arizona State University, who conducted unstructured interviews with 11 CIOs in Phoenix, Arizona. She found that CIOs see themselves as serving two major functions: general manager and manager of change. Boyle and Burbridge, who interviewed 14 CIOs in Maryland, assert that without the "authority and power to initiate corporate change, a CIO's resume is likely to reflect the recent 13% dismissal rate" (Boyle and Burbridge 1991, 13).

A New IS Relationship with Clients

In 1981, Ives and Olson found that the information managers they observed interacted with users only 10% of the time. However, they could not attribute this "noticeably absent" (Ives and Olson 1981, 49) interaction to Couger's finding that IS managers have low social needs. Information managers spent

79% using the verbal mediums compared to 78% for Mintzberg's (1973) CEOs and 80% for Stewart's (1976) middle managers. Furthermore, only 3% of the information content was technical.

The CIO must interact with other high-level officers of the company, but the information manager must also interact with other managers at his or her own functional level. Liaison activities are critical to the CIO and will become critical to other information resource managers and employees. Unlike the MIS managers observed a decade ago, the five CIOs observed in 1991 spent more time interacting with those outside the information technology group than those inside this group.

Reassignment of IS Employees

In 1980, Synnott recommended the Trojan horse approach to increasing interaction with users. He recommended sending IS groups out into the end-user organization. The state of Washington now sends "crews of programmers . . . into various . . . departments to handle multiple programming projects with end users. . . . We've reached the stage at which our mainframes are used basically as large data repositories. This is a major way we are restructuring" (Kolodziej 1989, 72). During the past few years, 500 of Amoco Corporation's 2000 corporate information systems employees have been assigned to client divisions.

A New Selection Criterion for IS Employees

At least one CIO has begun to use a new criterion for selection: "he has been hiring programmers who . . . do not have the baggage of a long history of mainframes behind them. Such programmers, he claims, are more apt to be open minded about new programming and IS organizational changes" (Kolodziej 1989, 73). One of the five CIOs observed interviewed every prospective employee, believing that this decision was strategic. During the interviews, he told them that their first training would be in the lighting business and that they had to know the business to be effective.

Successful CIO Characteristics a Model for IS Employees

As information systems become an integral part of every aspect of a company's business, the integration of the IS group has become essential. In fact, a 1989 Anderson Consulting survey of 120 IS executives in a range of *Fortune* 500 IS executives revealed that "communication with top management, functional managers, and end users" was the most frequently cited concern (92%) among the executives. O'Riordan (1987) identifies characteristics of the successful CIO:

- Being a business person
- Able to maintain an overall view of business needs
- Able to cross department boundaries and understand technology from a business perspective
- Innovative and flexible
- Able to communicate well.

These characteristics are also in demand for information managers and employees, who can no longer be isolated from the business. In today's environment, "contact . . . with functional management at their own level" must not be noticeably absent. Information technology units are now being restructured because of the widespread use of information technology. "We shape our tools, then they shape us " (Synnott 1987b, 339).

CONCLUSION

The growing importance of the top IS manager's job and the evolution of a new executive role are indicants of an even greater change—a change in the way we work, in the way we compete and communicate. According to Toffler (1990), the CIO is part of a major shift in the basis of power for organizations and for the global economy. For organizations in the near and distant future, the CIO's work is important not only to survive, but to prevail. Moreover, the CIO's work facilitates organizational restructuring by increasing the span of communication. Finally, the interaction patterns and business knowledge required for this work provide a paradigm for information systems work at all levels.

Since 1950, we have shaped our information technology tools. Now our information technology tools are shaping us. Whether an organization has a CIO or needs a CIO may reveal only one fact: whether that organization is in the mainstream of the global economy.

2

The CIO and Change

HOW IS THE CIO DIFFERENT FROM THE DATA PROCESSING OR MANAGEMENT INFORMATION SYSTEMS MANAGER?

Perhaps the most critical difference lies in the CIO's increased contact with top management and business unit managers. This contact, along with the CIO's technical expertise, enables him or her to function as a member of the strategy formulation team and to understand how information resources can be used to increase profitability and market share. The CIO must take the general rather than functional manager's approach and must act as an executive rather than a staff manager.

In 1979, Nolan (115) reported that "business needs a new breed of EDP [electronic data processing] manager." Nolan (1983) has suggested that information management is undergoing a transitional stage, one of technological discontinuity from traditional data processing (DP) technology, marked by mainframe computers, common software, and centralized data processing organizations, to a user-dominated technology, marked by distributed processing, the mainframe as a central repository, end-user computing, and decentralized information systems consultants in the operating units. Nolan sees increasing contact with functional units as part of the paradigm for end-user dominated technology.

While the MIS manager tended to report to finance/accounting and systems as well as the organization itself tended to centralized, the CIO is no longer tied to a single functional area. Organizations are working to decentralize themselves and their systems effectively. Involvement with information technology is occurring at the senior management level as innovative applications of technology are used to differentiate products and services. Information technology is an integral part of strategic planning as companies have moved beyond using technology to automate existing tasks and attain an efficiency or productivity advantage. Instead, organizations are using information technology to reengineer processes. Information technology has become the competitive weapon of choice. Telecommunications and computer technology have joined forces and information is viewed as a resource. Rather than an MIS manager who must focus on a fairly narrowly defined technical arena, the CIO must have a view of the whole organization if these resources are to be used to best advantage. Just as our systems have evolved from transaction processing systems which automate well defined tasks such as payroll, inventory, and accounts receivable, to systems which help senior managers make decisions, systems which facilitate the highest functions of managers, so has the scope of the information technology systems manager evolved. Instead of trying to control a well-defined project schedule, the CIO is trying to influence the direction of an organization and often times, the direction of an industry.

Table 2.1
Synnott's Summary of Eras and Roles

List of Characteristics	*Computer Era DP/MIS Manager*	**Information Era CIO**
Reports to	CFO	CEO
Organizational trend	centralized	decentralized
Management involvement	middle	senior
Manages	DP systems	information resources
Resource focus	computers	data and communication
Skills needed	technical	business management
Planning	technical	strategic
Technology focus	productivity	competitive advantage
Mission	control	technological innovation
Technology investment	conservative	aggressive
Technology integration	DP architecture	Information Resource Management architecture
Management style	control	influence

Synnott (1987a, 28) provides a succinct comparison of the roles for a DP or

Management Information Systems (MIS) manager and the CIO. The change in roles signals a change in eras.

WHAT ARE THE RESPONSIBILITIES OF THE CIO ROLE?

Since Synnott and Gruber's (1981) introduction of the role, prescriptive literature describing the responsibilities of this "superperson" has abounded. One survey has attempted to detail this role's responsibilities and the degree of responsibility (Brumm, 1988b). A study of the literature and surveys leads to consensus on the functions assigned to a CIO: information systems, telecommunications, computer operations, office automation, end-user computing/information center, and strategic planning. The following common CIO responsibilities were identified:

1. Policies, procedures, and standards for information resources
2. Strategic planning for information resources, linked to business planning, to provide improved organization functions and competitive advantage
3. Approval/acceptance of expenditures for information resources
4. Coordination of information technology units, functional units, and external or environmental units
5. Education of management, especially top management, on potential uses of information technology
6. Consulting services to business units and top management
7. Environmental scanning
8. Other general managerial work

Nolan (1979a, 1983) and Synnott (1987a,b,c) have noted the changing responsibilities for information executives. Nolan sees these responsibilities as a natural consequence of our move from traditional DP technology to user-dominated technology. The CIO facilitates, guides, and promotes change rather than controlling it.

3

Observing Five Successful CIOs

CIO SELECTION

Personal contacts and a literature search were used to identify five potential candidates. Following Mintzberg's (1973) model, five industry types were selected. The candidates were from insurance, higher education, manufacturing, a government agency, and utilities. A letter was sent to each candidate, followed by a phone call within two weeks. Surprisingly, all CIOs contacted agreed to be observed. They seemed intrigued by the study.

The criteria used for selecting these five CIOs were as follows:

- Highest ranking information technology executive in their organizations
- Report no more than two levels from CEO
- Responsible for information systems, computer operations, telecommunications, office automation, end user computing/information center
- Participates in strategic planning for the organization.

Preference was given to larger organizations, since Brown et al.'s (1988) study of 15 small to moderate size companies showed that their CIOs' involvement in strategic planning is questionable. One rule of thumb for size was that the information resource group be larger than 30 members. The actual range was 108-1384 members.

General indicants of success or effectiveness were also used for CIO selection. One CIO had received a Society for Information Management Partners in Excellence award and was Chairman of the Technical Committee of the Intelligent Building Institute. He served as an executive advisor and guest speaker for MIT's Sloan School of Business. Another was on the Advisory Board for the University of Georgia's Business School and was highly recommended by academic professionals familiar with his work. One was on the

Board of NeXT Computers and an advisor to the National Science Foundation. He had published over 30 articles on the use of information technology in higher education and is considered a leader in this field. The insurance company had been named one of the most innovative insurance companies of the year by *Forbes* magazine, largely due to its use of information technology. One CIO was recommended by academic professionals who had personal knowledge of the CIO's work with an extensive, international research network.

CIO PROFILES

The profile of the CIOs studied was compared to the 111 CIOs from *Fortune* 100 companies surveyed in Brumm's doctoral study (1988b) and was not dissimilar overall. These CIOs were white males, 54 years old on average, all married and all born in the United States. The five averaged 19 years of formal schooling, and three of the five holding a master's degree or Ph.D. Three of the five were hired from within for the position. The average length of time they had been CIO was 3.6 years. Two years following the study, all remained in their positions, and one was given additional international responsibility.

Only one of the five actually bore the title of CIO, and this only in combination with Vice President, the title of all but the government agency CIO. Similarly, all but this CIO reported to the President or an Executive Vice President. None of the CIOs reported to Finance.

These five CIOs seemed to agree to be observed because they were keenly interested in other CIOs and how the role was being performed in other organizations. Each CIO received a copy of observation results as part of the agreement to allow the observation.

THE PILOT STUDY

Prior to the CIO observation, a pilot study was conducted with a university academic computing manager. He held a doctorate in education and his specialization had been educational testing. The observation form and coding keys were revised several times during the pilot study, and the manager provided feedback on obtrusive and unobtrusive observation methods. A black notebook, with notepad on the right and black digital watch on the left, was used. Stapled observation coding forms allowed for easy but unobtrusive movement from coding form to notepad. Coding keys were clipped to the left side of the notebook for easy reference. Movement of paper and the observer's body position was minimized. The pilot study also allowed a test of the microcomputer database structure to ensure that all data necessary for the quantitative analysis had been captured.

Table 3.1
CIO Profiles

Title	Senior Vice President	Vice Provost	Senior Vice President	Director	Senior Vice Pres. & CIO
Type of Company	Insurance	University	Manufacturing	Government Agency	Utilities
Experience					
- as CIO	2 years	2 years	8 years	1.5 years	3 years
- with company	5 years	2 years	26 years	7 years	27 years
- in industry	20 years	22 years	26 years	15 years	27 years

Size
Insurance: annual revenues of $553 million, assets of $6 billion, 16 million Information Technology (IT) budget
University: information technology personnel budget $4.1 million annually
Manufacturing: annual sales of $600 million
Government Agency: annual budget of information systems division over $150 million
Utilities: annual revenues of $7.5 billion, assets of $20 billion

Following the pilot study, each organization was visited to gather preliminary data, meet key personnel, and glean a basic orientation to the CIO's work area. This orientation also involved a discussion of the CIO's work habits.

THE OBSERVATION WEEKS

An effort was made to schedule the observation during what the CIO and his administrative assistant deemed a typical week. A subsequent analysis of the primary way CIOs spend time, scheduled meetings, showed that the weeks were not atypical. That was also the judgment of the CIOs and administrative assistants. However, most CIOs remarked that a typical week did not exist.

Four of the five CIOs were observed for five continuous work days, which ensured that each day of the week was observed. During the observation at the manufacturing company, however, the CEO requested that the CIO make an unexpected, confidential trip on Thursday. A Thursday was rescheduled four weeks later, so this observation was not for five consecutive work days but did cover each day of the week.

Almost all coding took place on the day of observation, never longer than two days away from observation. I used every available opportunity for follow-up discussions, clarifications, and copies of documents, when needed for coding purposes. As did Mintzberg, I usually met with the CIO at the end of each work day to gain a better understanding of certain events and pieces of mail.

My experience as an industrial engineer and information systems manager was valuable for the structured observation of five CIOs. Ten years of experience in management also affected the observer's ability to make inferences regarding purpose, role, and responsibilities.

THE OBSERVER'S EFFECT

Mintzberg (1973) noted that after introductions and brief explanations, participants seemed to forget his presence quickly, and he believed that his presence had a minimal effect on the observation. Assessing the effect of the observer on the observed is difficult, especially when there is only one observer. My experience was similar to Mintzberg's. Most participants seemed to forget my presence after introductions. Remarkably candid and confidential meetings were conducted, tempers flared, and it appeared that business was conducted as usual. In only one meeting at the university did a participant seem unusually uncomfortable in my presence and addressed me directly during the meeting. The CIO then explained to this participant that if he acknowledged my presence in any way, he would affect the study negatively.

Whenever possible, I sat behind participants and out of the line of vision. Conversations were not taped because I considered that the ability to quote participants precisely was not as important as being unobtrusive. At the manufacturing company, the CEO insisted that I sit at the conference table with senior managers. He seemed to believe that it would be rude to exclude me. Avoiding eye contact was important in this situation. However, I had no sense that my presence affected the conduct of the meeting in any way.

During the five weeks, I observed 501 verbal contacts and 464 pieces of mail in 215 observation hours. Before describing the observation weeks (Chapters

5 through 9), in the following chapter I describe the analyses performed, including the meaning of variables coded. This description is a necessary prelude to the discussion of the day-to-day work life of the five successful CIOs.

4

The Observation Method

STRUCTURED OBSERVATION

Mintzberg (1973, Appendix B) surveyed seven common methods for studying managerial work:

1. Secondary methods
2. Questionnaire and interview
3. Critical incident and sequence of episodes
4. Diary
5. Activity sampling
6. Unstructured observation (narrative of events recorded)
7. Structured observation (activities coded and narrative of events recorded).

Structured observation was found to be inefficient when compared to all methods other than unstructured observation, yet Mintzberg found that only these two inefficient methods of study had allowed researchers to "understand new dimensions and to probe" (1973, 229). The advantages of unstructured observation are in-depth understanding and inductive development of theory. Structured observation adds the discipline of seeking prespecified data and studying quantifiable characteristics of work. Mintzberg compared this method to walking a tightrope. The observer seeks to balance too little structure, with the disadvantage that the research cannot be replicated, and too much structure, with the disadvantage that the observer may fail to develop a true understanding of events which are being researched precisely because they are not well understood.

Mintzberg's own observation categories have proved robust and have been used in fourteen replications of his study, in education, police work, and business (Ives and Olson 1981, Martinko and Gardner 1985). The use of coding categories allows the researcher a degree of comparability. However, Mintzberg emphasizes that structured observation goes beyond a mere categorizing of events, employing more of the anthropologist's approach: The "researcher is able to record detailed information on important incidents and to collect anecdotal materials" (1973, 232).

STRUCTURED OBSERVATION BEFORE AND AFTER MINTZBERG

Major findings from studies using structured observation before Mintzberg are as follows (Martinko and Gardner 1985):

- Managers experience high levels of activity, with brief contacts and many interruptions and with significant variation in activity levels and type of activity from manager to manager.

- Managers, at the apex of their organizational unit, must interact with members of the organization and members outside the unit. Much of this interaction is face to face or verbal.

- Relating performance level to the distribution of activity types has proved difficult. The complexity of measuring performance relative to each environment as well as inappropriate use of statistical analysis and differences in coding schemes have made the results with structured observation inconclusive. These studies have been fairly consistent in indicating that high performers tend to engage in activities of longer duration and have a lower activity level. While Martinko and Gardner (1985) conclude that these studies indicate that effective managers manage their time better, an alternative explanation is that the performance measure and an environment in which the manager can operate at a lower level of activity are confounded.

One of the most important results of these observations was to contradict "traditional academic depictions of the management and supervisory role" (Martinko and Gardner 1985, 684).

Mintzberg's study went beyond frequency distribution reports of previous studies and focused on the purpose of what was being done. Martinko and Gardner (1985, 684) find that his work also suggests that "brevity, variety, and fragmentation" increase as one moves down the management hierarchy and the importance of verbal interaction tends to increase as one moves up the hierarchy. They note (1985, 685), "Mintzberg's work represented an important methodological and theoretical breakthrough."

VARIABLES CODED

Mintzberg's Variable

Two types of data were recorded during observation: narrative or anecdotal and structured coded data. For verbal contacts, the medium, place, participants, initiation, duration, and purpose were recorded. The medium was categorized as a telephone call, unscheduled meeting, scheduled meeting, or tour. An unscheduled meeting is one arranged hastily or a drop-in. A tour is either a walkabout to observe or a chance discussion in the hall. Desk work involves written communication mediums: letters, reports, articles, memos, etc. Participants were coded by title categories. Initiation categories were either opposite (a participant), self, mutual, or clock (meaning regularly scheduled). A verbal contact lasted until a change in medium and/or participants occurred.

Desk work was coded as incoming or outgoing mail. For incoming mail, the form, sender, purpose, and type attention given was recorded. For outgoing mail, the target was noted. The major categories for form were letter, memo, clipping, report, and periodical. The title category of the sender and target was recorded as well. The type attention for incoming mail was coded as skim, read, study. The duration for each desk work session was recorded, but not the duration for each piece of mail. A desk work session lasted until a verbal contact interaction began.

Additional Variables

The CIO study replicates Mintzberg's, using the same variables or coding elements and operational definition of variables. Three major coding elements were added for the CIO study:

1. Mintzberg's managerial ten roles
2. The eight common CIO responsibilities
3. Group membership (external, functional, information technology).

Managerial Roles

The extent to which the CIO plays informational roles versus decisional roles is of interest in determining whether the work pattern is more like that of an executive or a staff specialist, more a managerial than technical role. Qualitative conclusions regarding CIOs compared to CEOs could be guided by a quantitative analysis of roles as well as anecdotal evidence. As Mintzberg emphasized, the roles are a gestalt and highly interrelated. Thus, the assignation of a primary role to each activity and piece of mail functioned as one element of "planned, methodical watching that involves constraints to improve accuracy" (Weick 1968, 358). Of course, more than one role sometimes applied to a contact or piece of mail. However, one primary role was assigned.

According to Mintzberg, managers play 10 roles, basically. These 10 roles can be grouped to form a triad, however. The triad within which these 10 roles are played are (1) interpersonal, (2) informational, and (3) decisional.

Mintzberg emphasized that his framework for describing managerial work required that a manager had been given formal authority and status by his or her organization.

Interpersonal roles include (1) leader, (2) liaison, and (3) figurehead. During any activity, the manager will serve as leader and/or liaison. According to Mintzberg (1975), activities involving those who are in the manager's vertical chain of command require a leader role. Activities involving those outside that vertical chain of command require that the manager play a liaison role. The figurehead role involves ceremonial duties such as greeting touring dignitaries, signing award certificates, attending a retirement dinner, etc.

Informational roles include (4) monitor, (5) disseminator, and (6) spokesperson. In the monitoring role, managers scan for or receive information. In the disseminator role, the manager gives information to subordinates. This information is often privileged information to which subordinates would not otherwise have access. As spokesperson, the manager speaks for the work unit managed either to another group, the direct report or superior, or those outside the organization itself.

Decisional roles include (7) entrepreneur, (8) disturbance handler, (9) resource allocator, and (10) negotiator. Mintzberg's (1975) definition of the entrepreneur role is that the manager playing this role seeks to improve the work unit and/or adapt it to changing environmental conditions. Many strategic planning sessions require this role. As a disturbance handler, the manager must deal with a crisis. The manager playing the role of resource allocator decides who gets what, including the allocation of the manager's own time. As negotiator, the manager negotiates for the work group. Importantly, the negotiator role has a prerequisite situation: The manager has resource allocation authority. Therefore, the negotiator and resource allocation roles are strongly linked.

Mintzberg's framework for managerial roles, developed several years after his observation of CEOs, was used as a coding element for the structured observation of CIOs. Two interpersonal roles, liaison and leader, applied to all activities and were identified by whether the CIO's contacts were outside or inside his unit. The remaining eight roles were used to code each verbal contact and piece of mail. The selection process for CIOs assured that all had been granted formal authority and status.

Responsibilities

The common responsibilities identified in the literature review were used to code activities:

- Policies, procedures, standards—guideline setting
- Strategic planning
- Approval/Acceptance of expenditures

- Coordination of three groups: IT, functional units, environment
- Education
- Consulting

One of the difficulties with this categorization is differentiating strategic planning from guideline setting, capital acquisitions, and consulting. Strategy planning involved those activities which occur prior to capital acquisition approval or acceptance and relate to specific projects rather than general guidelines or policy. A future orientation must be present as opposed to consulting on present problems.

Finally, activities were coded by a purpose category number and a subcategory letter, if applicable. While Mintzberg specified subcategories, he did not provide an analysis by these subcategories. Although these subcategories cannot be compared, they do provide valuable further description of activity purposes. Mintzberg used no title for an internal peer because the CEO had no internal peers. The peer title was made two titles for the CIO study: peer-external and peer-internal. The Director title, indicating the position to whom the CEO would report was used as the title for a superior or any participant, sender, or target who was at a rank higher than the CIO's in the organization. As in Mintzberg's study, the number of participants for each title code was indicated. The participant or sender's name was indicated on the coding form, so that if the title was unknown at the time, this information could be obtained later and a title code assigned.

The coding form also provided space for writing if time or familiarity with the organization did not allow for coding during observation. Two locations were added, home and a peer's office. Other locations, coded by number as were titles, are as follows:

- Manager's office
- Subordinate's office
- Superior's office
- Hall
- Plant
- Conference room
- Board room
- Away from the organization

The "plant" location was the organization's facilities at large (i.e., not in an office, conference room, or hall). The computer operations area, the manufacturing processes, and the network control area were coded as "plant." No location for the CIO's automobile was added, although car phones were used. This location was written on the form and the number for "away from organization" was assigned. Likewise, one CIO had a table reserved at a local restaurant for lunch. There, he conducted business using a portable phone, as if he were in his office. The "away from organization" code was applied here as well.

Comparability with Mintzberg's (1973) and Ives and Olson's (1981) study encouraged a literal application of location codes. Mintzberg assumed the location for desk work to be the manager's office and, therefore, did not analyze desk work location. Location was coded for desk work as well as for verbal contacts and analyzed for both, because CIOs processed mail in a variety of locations (airplanes, taxis, administrative assistant's office with guidance, subordinate's office, restaurant).

Mail categories (letter, memo, clipping, report, periodical) were supplemented with a code for electronic mail. All other medium categories were coded with an "E" as well, when applicable. A piece of mail received or sent from a fax machine was coded with the suffix "fx." Although categorized under the mail short form, memos (for comparison with Mintzberg), authorization forms requiring quick processing (travel expense approval, low-level expenses or acquisitions) were coded "AF." The observer experienced a sufficient number of these authorizations to constitute a separate category. Books were also added as a desk work form category.

For verbal contact mediums, telephone calls and conference calls were distinguished by coding ("C" and "CC"), but both were analyzed as calls when comparing to Mintzberg. A videoconference was coded as a scheduled meeting, but videoconference was noted on the coding form. Voice mail was coded as a call, but the suffix "v" was added as well.

A description of a week in the life of five CIOs follows. The work is placed in context, with a background for the organization and IT group. The analysis of each CIO's activities includes:

- Chronology record or how the CIO spends his (all CIOs were male) time
- Responsibilities
- Managerial roles.

These analyses all provide different ways of viewing the CIOs' work. Names of organizations and CIOs are not given to protect privacy since intimate details of work life are discussed. Organizations are given aliases, however. I must emphasize that direct quotations attributed to participants may not be precise since the conversations were not recorded. Direct quotations which are observation dialogue should be considered as paraphrases based upon notes taken during the observations.

5

The University CIO

BACKGROUND

University

Evergreen University (an alias) is a well-endowed private institution located in a major Southern city. It has 4300 undergraduate students and 4700 graduate students. The undergraduate program is liberal arts oriented and the graduate program is dominated by a nationally known medical program. The university is affiliated with a Protestant church and retains what might be described as a Southern aristocratic culture. Because of the hospital and medical center associated with the medical school, the university is the third largest employer in the city. The medical school operates with a great deal of autonomy and has its own administrative information systems for the operation of the school, hospital, and research centers. The President oversees what might be compared to two subsidiaries: the undergraduate program and the medical complex.

Evergreen is aggressively seeking national recognition. A recent raid on John Hopkins's French department made headlines. Other nationally known professors were hired in physics, and a search was being made in biology. With an endowment of $923 million, the twelfth largest in the nation, the university can afford this aggressive strategy.

One facet of this aggressive strategy was to implement Carnegie-Mellon's strategy of becoming a computer-intensive institution. Every student, regardless of major, becomes well grounded in information technology. As part of this strategic thrust, a Vice Provost for Information Technology was recruited two years ago. This Vice Provost has functional responsibility for Academic Computing (student labs, consulting, software, Faculty Information Technology Center), Business Affairs (budget), Information Systems (finance, student, employee, library, and departmental computing), Microcomputer Support (consulting, repair, local area networks, acquisitions), Technical Services (operations, network services, production control, operating systems), telecommunications, and research and planning. This CIO brought over 20 years of experience in information technology at three educational institutions to the university. Two of these institutions also had medical schools. More importantly, he brought a strong commitment to the strategy of making the university a computer-intensive institution. In an article entitled "The Computer Revolution and Graduate Education," he echoes Donovan's (1989, 84) pronouncement that the issue is survival: "What is at stake is not efficiency. What is at stake is survival." In another article, he states, "While the use of computers for research and administrative duties may be a by-product . . . in a computer intensive environment, the central effort must be on undergraduate learning."

The Vice Provost of Information Technology for the university reports to the Provost for Academic Affairs, who in turn reports to the university President. Also reporting to the Provost are all deans, the library, and administration. Peers of the Provost are the Executive Vice President (Finance and Operations) and the Vice President of Health Affairs. Information Technology had formerly reported to the Executive Vice President (Finance and Operations). The new CIO or Vice Provost of IT was placed in the academic and administrative mainstream, with finance being one of the Information Technology Division's (ITD) clients. The new CIO also was designated as having a dotted line relationship with Health Affairs and thus provided advisory assistance.

The new CIO lists 30 papers and publications on his vita and has presented "over 60 keynote addresses and presentations on information technology to colleges, universities, government agencies, and professional associations during the past five years."[1] His views were well known to the university when they recruited him:

The new information technology presents education with two challenges. First, students must be prepared for a world that, because of intelligent machines, will require different intellectual skills. Second, the new information technology offers ways of changing the learning process itself. In other words, the new technology affects what we learn and how we learn. Until recently, the what's and how's have been attacked as two distinct problems by different academic groups.

The university CIO believes in the integration of information technology throughout academic and administrative functions. He believes that to "escape the process" of the leader strategy even though it is a risky process, is also to "escape many gains."

---

[1] All quotations, unless identified otherwise, are from the study I conducted or from written materials, such as this Curriculum Vita, which if cited, would violate the study's agreement of anonymity.

According to the university CIO, " Leaders have learning experiences that are not easily transferred to others . . . In the process of trying, taking risks, evaluating and trying again, people develop and grow . . . leading is exhilarating and creates an atmosphere of experimentation and change characteristic of excellent organizations." Effecting change, according to this CIO, requires a "command of resources, and the only way to command resources in most universities is to have line responsibility."

Because he has been a leader in integrating information technology, this CIO has learned the risks of the job and the reasons for high turnover in the position:

People in these new positions are changing the organizational and power structure of the university. Today, the typical senior information technology officer has responsibility for academic computing, administrative computing, telephones, and the communications system. In the past, these responsibilities were the charge of various vice presidents and officers . . . [and] rather than being all powerful [the CIO] is often in the tenuous position of having responsibility but struggling for authority that has been wrested from others.

He also cites the dual role which a CIO must play "the new officer must be a Jekyll and Hyde. On campus his effort must be low keyed, to create a level of expectation that allows for the possibility of success. Off campus, he must be a promoter and visionary." He finds "high expectation" to be the greatest advantage and disadvantage: It drives change but can force failure.

The university's Vice Provost for IT is on the University Advisory Panel for the NeXT Computer Corporation is an advisor and reviewer for the National Science Foundation, and is on the advisory panel for the office of Technology Assessment of Congress, the Board of Trustees for EDUCOM (Interuniversity Communications Council), and the editorial board of two journals dealing with computers and education. He has also served in an advisory capacity for several colleges and universities, including the University of Alabama at Birmingham, University of Arizona, University of Colorado, and the American Association of Medical Colleges.

Information Technology Division

The Information Technology Division (ITD), the CIO's organizational unit, is designed "to help people in the [university] community use modern information technology to improve teaching, research, and public service. The emphasis is on people (students, faculty, and staff) rather than information technology (computers, telephones, and data bases)." The ITD believes that current and future information technology can directly improve the quality of scholarly activity at [the university]. It helps in mundane yet important ways by efficiently registering students, processing admissions, keeping track of budgets,

and getting out payroll checks. And increasingly, it cuts to the core of intellectual activity by stimulating the imagination, reformulating information, and
enhancing communications. No disciplinary area will be untouched by information technology over the next decade.

This mission was set forth by the CIO in the monthly ITD magazine distributed throughout the campus. The CIO writes a column for this publication. As
he sees it, the "unique challenge" at this university is "to assure that information
technology is used to enhance and not destroy our humane traditions."

The ITD employs approximately 130 people. Microcomputer Support services
a base of over 3000 personal computer systems. Network Services must
monitor over 2500 connections on the campus data network. Telecommunications has responsibility for over 9000 telephone lines at the university and
hospital. Technical Services operates equipment worth more than $6 million.
Output from this operation is between 3 and 4 million pages each month.
Library Automation maintains an electronic catalog with over 540,000 entries
and provides search capability for a variety of databases. Information Services
programs and maintains both administrative and academic systems. Academic
computing also supports 78 different software packages and answers approximately 3100 consulting calls each year. In addition, it teaches 180 short courses
each year.

ITD has a joint venture with the library, the Faculty Information Technology
Center (FITC), which is located in the library and staffed by members of
Academic Computing. Its mission is "to familiarize . . . faculty with the latest
information technology that may be used in teaching and scholarly research,"
according to the CIO in his monthly column. Members of the ITD will "help
faculty to apply innovative technologies." An example of a useful technology
in the Center is the IBYCUS computer which provides full text searches of
Thesaurus Linguae Graecae and *Thesaurus Linguae Latinea*, both representing
a large collection of Greek, Latin, and Biblical texts from 800 B.C. to 700 A.D.

The FITC is one of four projects which the CIO cites as exhibiting the three
characteristics of IT projects in an academic environment:

1.   They are joint ventures which cut across organizational boundaries
2.   They merge media types such as videos and computers to create innovative
     solutions
3.   They emphasize what people are trying to do versus what technology can be
     used to do.

Information technology adoption in universities seems to be entering the third
of what the CIO has described as the pattern for technology adoption. First,
technology automates manual activities. Second, technology creates new
applications, things that were never done before manually. Third, technology
changes lifestyles.   The lifestyle of students and teachers/researchers is

beginning to be affected. The same is true for members of the ITD.

Within the division, the CIO perceives two cultures at war: that of the veteran "DP types" from the days when administrative computing reported to finance and that of the more academically oriented and trained information systems professionals, who believe in development methodologies and entity modeling, data dictionaries, and prototypes. While this second group is accustomed to mainframe systems, it is not trapped in a mainframe mentality. One system employing cooperative processing is currently in implementation and clients are part of the project team, not adversaries of the project team. The CIO has been working to shift the culture toward the second group. A major obstacle is that those with the longest seniority and power within the organization are in the first group.

Turnover has already occurred in the position next in command to the CIO's, and the CIO has chosen not to fill the position immediately. What he describes as "an unfreezing" has resulted, but conflict still exists. Another strategy the CIO has implemented is to represent deliberately the client's view within the ITD. His response to a complaint that the business school was performing functions that should be performed on a charge-back basis by the computer center was, "My purpose is not to build a computer center, but to enhance computing on campus. Does this enhance computing on campus?"

Conflict existed within the division and between the division and its clients. Much of this functional conflict seemed due to what the CIO has described as a wresting of power from functional areas when the division was organized. Resistance to this change had not been overcome completely. Potential conflicts existed in the academic arena as well. A computing fee had been added to student tuition. The ITD division will have a major voice in the allocation of these funds to different departments. These departments may disagree with decisions made, especially if the decision is perceived to be disadvantageous to their department. Moreover, the academics are accustomed to relative autonomy regarding instructional resource decisions.

The ITD is geographically dispersed, but the majority of the division members are in one building. The CIO is not in this building but is in the administrative building along with the Provost and President.

THE OBSERVATION WEEK

The CIO retained the working hours of academic life, working at home each night and keeping flexible office hours. This flexibility, as well as some protection from daily operating details and mail, was afforded by the presence of a capable administrative assistant. She screened his mail, took phone calls, handled many of the phone calls, monitored situations on campus and within ITD, and acted as a sounding board for many of his ideas. A Southerner involved in state political activities at a high level, she was often able to interpret actions or comments for the CIO, who was a Northerner from an urban background. He had grown up in a Jewish neighborhood where he was the minority, so he was accustomed to cultural differences and acutely aware of their importance.

The administrative assistant knew the university, its culture, and, according to the CIO, "how things happen." She described the CIO as a high-energy person who must have quiet time to concentrate. Otherwise, he would gravitate toward personal interaction. She controlled his calendar at his request. All requests for his time went through her, and she "played the heavy." According to the administrative assistant, the CIO's style was not the university's style, but the university needed the change that he represented. Nevertheless, presentation of that change must not be too radical. The current President was a minister and former missionary. While the CIO might not fit the mold of what has been a conservative university, he must not be perceived to vary far from it.

The administrative assistant described the CIO as a creative person and a risk taker. Every Saturday morning, she cleaned his office and prioritized what remained to be done, and they met every morning for a review. In her words, she "kept the train on the track," but in no way patronized the CIO. They worked as partners. She described him as a person who knows "the importance of spirit, of people feeling that what they do matters. He is well read, sees connections, relations. He does not have tunnel vision."

Chronology Record

The CIO exercised at lunch and found this an excellent opportunity to become acquainted with faculty members and university personnel on an informal basis, thus facilitating better working relationships. He also found this an excellent way to monitor events on campus and to learn the politics of campus life. During the observation week, the CIO spent 51% of his time on desk work (Appendix A). He was the only CIO for whom the written medium was equal to the verbal contact mediums. Of that 51% of desk work time, 21% was accomplished at home, with the CIO conscientiously providing all coding element information as well as a brief description of the purpose for mail.

Verbal Contacts

Forty-eight percent of the CIO's verbal contacts were with subordinates and 13% with clients. He was involved with two projects, a human resource management system and a fund-raising system. The fund-raising system was of strategic importance because it provided a model for future development. It used IBM's relational database, DB2, on the mainframe with microcomputers at client workstations in the client-server model. Most importantly, the discipline of a methodology had been imposed with entity modeling, data dictionaries, and prototyping. Client involvement had been high, and the systems group had learned the client's business. The client project leader also commented that this methodology had caused the fund raising group in Development to understand their business much better.

The human resources system, on the other hand, had been plagued by conflict and political struggles. A breakdown in communications had occurred between the clients and ITD project group. The CIO's involvement was required. The turnover in his deputy's post and the CIO's decision not to fill the post immediately caused these kinds of conflicts to come directly to the CIO.

The CIO initiated 40% of his verbal contacts, and the opposite party initiated 43%; the contact was mutual 13% of the time and regularly scheduled or by the clock 4% of the time. Sixty-five percent of the contact occurrences were in the CIO's office. The CIO's office also had a small, circular conference table which could accommodate most of his meetings. Fifty percent of his scheduled meetings and 97% of his unscheduled meetings were one-on-one meetings. However, 30% of his meetings involved more than four people.

Using Mintzberg's purpose categories to analyze contact time, the university CIO spent only 18% of his time on strategy compared to 31% on average. That he was implementing a strategy and reshaping the ITD to fit that strategy was clear. However, he did not attend scheduled meetings which were overtly devoted to strategy formulation, as did other CIOs.

Incoming Mail

Incoming mail (Appendix A.3) was usually in the form of memos (51%) and was from subordinates (54%). Eleven percent was received from clients. Twenty-three percent of incoming mail was in the form of letters and 15% in the form of reports. The university CIO received four books (7% of mail) during the week. Only one other CIO received a book. Twenty-eight percent of the incoming mail was requests or decisional and 72% was information.

Outgoing Mail

The university CIO initiated 73% of the CIO's output as opposed to reacting to inputs. Forty-seven percent of outgoing mail occurrences was in the form of reports; 33%, memos; and 16%, letters. Major targets of the outgoing mail were as follows: subordinates (33%), peers-external (33%), superiors (15%), peer-internal (9%).

The CIO worked on the University of Wisconsin report, which consisted of many sections, throughout the week. This report accounts for the high percentage of reports and external targets (12 of 21 report occurrences).   Written preparation for oral presentations was also coded report.   Mintzberg had no separate category for presentation preparation.   Any speaking situation for this CIO was preceded by written preparation.   To prepare for the President's tour of the Faculty Information Technology Center, the CIO prepared a written guide for his conversation ahead of time.   Before staff meetings, he composed a written form of his verbal agenda.   He prepared his oral report on two National Science Foundation proposals in written form.   Called upon to make an impromptu speech at a service awards banquet, he sketched an outline quickly on the back of an envelope.

The CIO told me that written preparation not only improved his delivery but also focused his attention so he could deliver his views more energetically and convincingly.   Verbal contacts were often prepared for and followed up with desk work sessions.   Writing was a means of thinking, rethinking, and clarifying communication.   After a policy meeting with the human resources manager, the CIO stated in a letter what he understood the policy to be.   He encouraged the use of the written medium in project work as well to clarify project status and coming events.

Mintzberg's purpose categories for output describe what kind of response is being made rather than why the response is being made.   Thirty-one percent of the CIO's output was a reply to a written request or information received (Appendix B.4).   Nine percent of the output involved forwarding information to subordinates.   The location for desk work (Appendix D.2) was in the manager's office (75%) and at home (21%).   Only the manufacturing CIO, who used his home office for quiet time, did more of his desk work at home.

Interaction Analysis

Desk work was divided fairly evenly among the three interaction groups: external to the organization, IT unit, and functional groups outside the IT unit but within the organization.   The split between non-IT areas and IT was also about 50-50 in terms of verbal contact time (Appendix H.7).

Responsibility Analysis

Verbal Contacts

An analysis of activities by the common responsibility areas (Appendix E) shows that the university CIO spent more of his verbal contact time in environmental scanning activities than other CIOs.   He commented that universities had enjoyed freer access to other universities and vendors than corporations because they had been viewed as noncompetitive.   That view is now changing, he believes, and he has found that many educational institutions are becoming reluctant to share information, particularly about successful IT implementations.

Over half of the verbal contacts can be accounted for by responsibilities: coordination of the three groups, other general managerial, and consulting on present problems. Only the government agency CIO spent less time on strategic planning. Both the utility and government agency CIOs spent higher percentages of verbal time on policies, procedures, and guidelines, however.

Desk Work

A responsibility analysis of desk work (Appendix E.2) shows that coordination of the three areas is the highest percentage of occurrences for the written and verbal contact mediums. However, environmental scanning ranked second for pieces of mail. Other general managerial and strategic planning both represent 13% of the mail, and policies and procedures represent 10%.

Roles Analysis

Verbal Contacts

In addition to assigning each verbal contact and piece of mail to a responsibility area, Mintzberg's roles were assigned (Appendix F.1-F.10) to augment the purpose analysis and to provide a comprehensive view of the CIO role in terms of Mintzberg's managerial roles framework. For the university CIO, verbal interaction involved informational roles 10% of the contact time and decisional roles 83% of the contact time. The contact occurrence distribution is close to that of desk work wherein informational roles occurred 29%; decisional roles, 70%; and figurehead, 1%. The dominant decisional role for verbal contacts is disturbance handler, with 40% of contacts and 45% of time devoted to this role. Although resource allocator accounts for 28% of contacts, it consumed only 14% of contact time. Entrepreneurial activities, on the other hand, account for only 7% of the CIO's contacts but for 18% of his time. None of the informational roles were greater than 7% on an occurrence or a time basis. This CIO's verbal contacts were dominated by decisional roles.

Disturbance handling seemed to be required by the highly political nature of some conflicts and by the split within the ITD between DP types and information systems professionals discussed earlier. The human resources system was sensitive because the client group reported to the Executive Vice President for Finance and Operations. Many in the development group had formerly reported to Finance and felt that some of the clients had a vested political interest in sabotaging the project. Half of disturbance handling related to this project.

The problems with this project had become so severe that the CIO had employed the services of an outside consultant with no political interests in the matter to observe and report to him and the university. He realized that the project could not be turned into a power play or he would be the loser. The conflict must be neutralized and the outside consultant could at least document for the Provost and the President what problems existed and the source of the problems. Further complicating this project was the fact that the DP-type members of the division seemed to want the draw the CIO into the fray. They also perceived the CIO and the new culture as a threat, just as the new structure had evoked lingering opposition from Finance.

The consultant told me that his main value to the university might be to assure it that the political conflicts of this project were common in his experience over the past three years and that particular people were not to blame. Specifically, turnover in the CIO position would not be a quick fix to the problem, although many organizations tend to try this first, he said. Often this is the remedy urged by powerful executives who have had some power wrested from them during a restructuring of the IT function, he continued. Often these executives are firmly positioned, with years of experience at the organization, whereas the CIO may be a newcomer, which was the case at the university.

Two project meetings and a series of meetings about a personnel conflict embody the nature of the CIO's disturbance handling role. This role consumed 47% of his scheduled meeting time, 49% of his unscheduled meeting time, and 35% of his telephone time.

The CIO used the fund-raising project as the counterpoint to the human resources project both within the ITD, with the Finance group, and with the Provost and President. He emphasized that this project was significant as a demonstration of what could be done. He told me after the fund-raising project meeting that a CIO can not survive if two of these three groups is against him: superiors, clients, information technology unit. This project would give him the support of two immediately (superiors and clients) and in the long term, the information technology unit. He added that it doesn't pay to make enemies anywhere, even with the janitor. On the other hand, he said, "my experience is that I often have to change behavior to change attitudes."

The fund-raising project meeting was attended by the VP of Development and the VP of Health Affairs, the client manager for the project, the ITD project leader, the Assistant VP of Development, the Director of Administrative Computing, and several ITD project team members. The VP of Health Affairs reported directly to the President and had responsibility for all divisions of the medical school and its hospitals and research centers.

The client manager and ITD project leader reviewed project status and upcoming events. The atmosphere was pleasant, and laughter came easily to participants. The client manager and project leader agreed that the single most important decision was not just to add a module to an already patched system, but to change the entire model upon which the system was based. The thrust of analysis had been to identify the information needed to do business rather than needed to do reports. The project used IBM's database, DB2, entity modeling, prototyping, and cooperative processing. The VP of Development commented on how useful the documentation had been to him in managing the area. People within the area had been using the same words but discussing different concepts. He agreed with the client manager that 10 years from now, they would not be in the same position as they were today: trying to use a patched system lacking adequate documentation.

While we were walking back from this meeting, the CIO commented that the timing of the two project meetings was critical. The good project presentation needed to occur first. The fund-raising or donor system meeting occurred Tuesday afternoon and the human resource system meeting Thursday afternoon. Wednesday afternoon, another successful project was demonstrated in the library, and this demonstration was attended by faculty representatives.

The human resources project meeting was not attended by the Executive VP for Finance and Operations. Instead, he sent two subordinates, the VP of Finance and the Treasurer. The ITD project manager, the Director of Administrative Computing, the personnel manager, the Vice President of Development, and the consultant attended. During the meeting, the CIO often translated what the ITD project leader and Director of Administrative Computing said. Reference was made to a DBD. The VP of Finance asked, "What's a DBD?" The CIO explained that a database dictionary is a critical concept. He quoted the VP of Development at the donor system meeting: "If we had only the data dictionary from the project, the project would have been worthwhile."

The CIO pushed the issue of a freeze date. When the VP of Finance responded that they were trying to freeze the specifications, the CIO told a Knute Rockne (Notre Dame football coach) story about 11 guys trying to beat Army versus 11 guys doing it. He emphasized that freezing the specifications is a critical point in projects, a cathartic experience during which intense conflict is common. He emphasized that everyone must understand that there was no alternative. He used the analogy of playing mixed doubles in tennis with one's spouse. It's too late to improve the spouse's game; all one can do is provide encouragement and support. "And remember that you've got to sleep with her that night." While laughter was still subsiding, he forged ahead. A major problem with the project was that negative statements were constantly made to the Executive VP of Finance, who then passed these statements on. He reminded clients that they were not budgeted for a perfect system, nor could a system be customized easily without a database and fourth-generation language. Finance had opted to modify an existing system, but the required modifications continued to multiply.

The CIO steered comments such as "from a DP point of view" and "we need user time to get it right" toward a discussion of what could realistically be expected by when and dealt with sources of conflict openly. His effort was to avoid an emotional or biased approach. He also mentioned that the library staff had requested that the counseling staff work with them on coping with change when the successful new system was implemented there.

Another example of disturbance handling was a series of meetings involving a conflict between two administrative assistants. One administrative assistant requested a conference with the CIO because she was unsatisfied with the results from other conferences. She was not comfortable with the fact that assignments which she thought were in her territory were being handled by the other administrative assistant. Her territory broadly defined was personnel administration for ITD. However, the CIO had enlisted the other administrative assistant to draft the ITD employee policy manual.

The basis of his decision had not been chain of command but individual characteristics, fitting the person to the assignment. He was particularly sensitive to words such as supervisor or user and wanted a teamwork approach rather than a hierarchical or bureaucratic approach to be conveyed through the language of the policy manual. The administrative assistant chosen for the task had that approach and was an imaginative person whom the CIO described as being "underdeployed" at present.

The conflict between the two assistants had been discussed at the biweekly staff meeting. The conflict seemed to have become symbolic of the conflict within the ITD group, between the old and new way. The conflict had assumed more importance than could be assigned to it merely on its own merits. The CIO used the discussion of this conflict to explain his approach and why he chose the person for the task at hand. He avoided discussion of the details and focused instead on why this conflict had become so important. He explained to the managers that the administrative assistant chosen was enthusiastic, positive, understood nonadversarial relationships, and showed initiative. If that sometimes made her difficult to work with because she stepped into other's territory, then the concept of territory needed to be reexamined in view of the group's objectives.

During the meeting with the administrative assistant who felt she had been slighted, the CIO focused on her strong points and her value to the organization. He reiterated that his approach was to avoid "boss" or territorial relationships and encourage a more decentralized, teamwork approach.

In the verbal contact mediums, the university CIO used the disturbance handler role to effect change within and outside the ITD. These changes were essential to long term strategic plans for information system methodologies, the ITD organization and culture, and the integration of information technology with the mainstream of campus life. Events precipitated disturbance handling, but the low percentage of time when the entrepreneur role was the primary role is deceiving. The CIO seized disturbance handling necessities as opportunities for improving and changing the ITD and the university's use of information technology.

Desk Work

An analysis of desk work shows that the dominant role of outgoing desk work was entrepreneur (42%). Resource allocator ranked second (24%) and the spokesperson role third (16%). The three roles—entrepreneur, resource allocator, spokesperson—accounted for 82% of outgoing mail. Only one other CIO had a higher percentage of outgoing mail devoted to the entrepreneur role: the manufacturing CIO with 50%. Both the university and manufacturing CIO used the uninterrupted time in a home office for much of this desk work. The university CIO's main entrepreneurial project was a report for the University of Wisconsin. This report evaluated Wisconsin's current status and made recommendations on how the university could move to a computer-intensive environment. Although this report was seemingly an external entrepreneurial activity, much of the consideration could be applied directly to the CIO's university and was a way of presenting these findings in a nonthreatening way to the university's administration. He had approval to do this study, and the administration was interested in this joint effort with a noncompetitive institution. The report would be read at the CIO's university as well as at Wisconsin.

Desk work coming in (Appendix F.6) required resource allocation (33%), monitoring (21%), disturbance handling (20%), and entrepreneurial roles (15%). The resource allocator role was lower than for all but the utility CIO. At the time of the observation, the utility CIO did not have to approve capital expenditures for the operating companies. A restructuring project in progress would change that requirement and the utility CIO's resource allocation role. Other CIOs experienced 50, 53, and 63% of their incoming mail as a resource allocation role. Again, the disturbance handling role was exceptionally high, as with verbal contacts, 20% compared to 2, 3, 3, and 3% for other CIOs. The entrepreneurial role for incoming mail was also high, as it was with outgoing mail.

The university CIO was actively pursuing change, using both the disturbance handler role in verbal contact mediums and the entrepreneur role for desk work. With the new funds from the computer fees, the research allocator role should become more important.

Verbal Contacts and Desk Work

Using all occurrences of desk work and verbal contacts (Appendix F.8), the university CIO played decisional roles in 73% of occurrences; informational roles, 25%; and figurehead, 2%. The leader role within the ITD (Appendix H. 7) was played for 54% of verbal occurrences. The liaison role with function areas and the environment was played for 46% of verbal occurrences and 63% of all desk work (Appendix D.1). The leader and liaison roles seemed to be of equal importance for the university CIO.

6

The Manufacturing CIO

BACKGROUND

Industry

The commercial and industrial lighting market is dominated by nine companies, who together control 50% of the over $4 billion market. The manufacturing company observed is the number one company in the market and has one close competitor in the over $500 million in sales category. In the 1980s, a series of acquisitions and mergers reduced the number of lighting companies, leaving only one third the number existing in the 1960s. The giants remaining offered a wide variety of lighting products, striving to gain contracts for the entire package of lighting used in a construction project.

The manufacturing CIO, speaking to a local meeting of the Society for Information Management (SIM), identified four critical success factors for the lighting industry:

One is product; that is what kinds of products—a broad or narrow product line—do we have. Two is price as it relates to the competition. Three is availability; that is, do we make an inventory of standard items available to the local distributors and contractor and how fast can we get our customers nonstandard fixtures from one of our factories as compared to our competitors availability. Four is service; how do we stack up one competitor to the other in the service we give to our customers.

In the lighting industry, independent agents who employ marketing representatives earn commissions on products sold. They usually have exclusive rights to a company's products within a given territory and cannot carry competing products. Agents act as the primary interface between the lighting company and the market. They have gradually assumed many of the roles, particularly that of providing technical expertise, played by the distributors in the 1960s and 1970s. As lighting companies grew larger and offered a wider range of lighting products, the agent became capable of providing the entire job package. Agents now define what products are needed for a job, price the products and apply their own commissions, and place orders for products. Agents know the local markets and cultivate relationships with local contractors and specifiers. The distributor, who had assembled a package for a contractor by contacting many agents, now primarily provides readily available inventory and financing to contractors. Stock items are inventoried at independent warehouses, but customized products must be ordered from the company's product division.

Once a quote is converted to an order, communication regarding order status and shipping dates is required so that the contractor can effectively schedule labor at the job site. The high degree of coordination required in the construction industry makes information and timely communication of that information a valuable service. Thus, access to that information gives an agent a competitive advantage.

COMPANY

Lilbourne Lighting (an alias) is organized by product group divisions. Three of the six Senior Vice Presidents head product group divisions. The President and the Senior Vice Presidents are known as the "Seniors" or the "Senior Seven." The Chief Information Officer (CIO) role is assigned to the Senior Vice President of one of these product group divisions: Management, Information, and Electronic Systems (MIES). In addition to his responsibility for Information and Management Services (I & MS), he is responsible for the Controls, Emergency Systems, and Reloc (relocatable lighting) product divisions.

The Fluorescent division is the oldest division and is the world's largest manufacturer of fluorescent lighting fixtures. Lilbourne Lighting (LL) was founded as a manufacturer of fluorescent fixtures in 1946. The Hi-Tek division was established in 1971 to capture a new and growing market: high-intensity discharge lighting. Begun as a result of a lighting market analysis, the group was led by a manager who had been responsible for Materials Management and Information Systems. The present CIO had reported to this manager at that time. Through new product development and acquisitions, the manufacturing company came to offer products for most segments of the commercial lighting market. LL has 3.3 million square feet of facility space and 13 manufacturing sites in six states and in Canada. Total employment exceeds 5000 and a large percentage of these employees have been members of the team for over 10 years.

MANAGEMENT, INFORMATION, AND ELECTRONIC SYSTEMS (MIES)

The VP of Information and Management Systems (I&MS), who reports to the CIO, has four direct reports: Director of Data Processing, Director of Information Systems, Manager of Systems Training, and Systems Engineering. Data Processing is responsible for operations, hardware services, and communications. Information Systems is responsible for application systems, internally and in the field. Training includes field training for market entities (agents, distributors, specifiers, warehouses, and contractors), internal systems training, and a support line for the field and within the company. Field system implementation, support, and training had previously reported to a VP of Management Services. Other functions reported to a VP of Information Systems. The former VP of Management Services is now the VP of a product division, Controls, and the two areas have been consolidated.

Of these four direct reports to the VP of I&MS, two positions were open due to a separation and a resignation. The CIO commented that people at LL did not understand how he could have let the Director of Data Processing be separated. He was a well-liked, long-term member of the family. The Systems Engineering position had become open during the last month due to a resignation. The Manager of Systems Training position had been open due to turnover, but was filled by promotion from within during the last year.

As LL headed toward the $1 billion in sales mark, volumes increased, new systems were added, and old systems were enhanced. Many of these systems were mission critical, that is, the company simply could not do business without them. Therefore, the pressures experienced by the I&MS group intensified with the company's growth.

Each market entity's systems were connected through a data communication network called LightLink. Work on a new contractor system, CALL (Contractor Access to Lilbourne Lighting) was in progress. This network was a primary reason for the CIO and CEO SIM Partners Leadership award. Excerpts from the nomination speech follow:

In 1976, Lilbourne Lighting embarked on an explicit strategy of improving its competitive posture—long before it was popular to talk of using information technology to gain competitive advantage. The central feature of the strategy . . . was to increase sales and profit level by posturing Lilbourne in a manner that enabled it to be a company that was "easy to do business with" and to deliver the "best value in lighting." . . . During the following seven year period over which LightLink evolved, Lilbourne invested $5 million and added to its staff individuals with unique expertise in underlying technology critical to the system plan.

LightLink could not have emerged as an information systems project without the partnership between [the CEO] and [the CIO]. It was not an information systems project, it was a top level, yet fundamental, business strategy. It was a corporate commitment. [The CIO] became the catalyst that forged information technology enabling the firm to pursue its strategy . . . When the LightLink vision was being created, the quality of data communication services had not yet advanced to current levels. Vendors were not able to offer adequate business solutions.

[The CIO] recognized early on that personal computers could become an awesome competitive weapon for Lilbourne and its agents if the appropriate network of support systems was established. The decision and the commitment to proceed occurred before the IBM PC had become the industry standard (and while many corporate staff members considered PC's to be nothing more than toys). Personal computers, along with computer networking became the means of linking agents, specifiers, etc. into the LightLink system.

Instead of using jargon, LightLink systems were named with acronyms which made sense. Agents were provided with an ACE in the marketplace—an Agency Communications Environment for processing orders, determining order status, and generating engineering layouts and calculations. They were also provided agency management systems, including training for using widely available microcomputer software such as spreadsheets and word processing. LightLink raised switching costs. Likewise, field warehouses were given help by SOS, a Stock Order System.

While these field systems were being developed and enhanced (ACE+, SOS+), two programs for internal systems were begun. The CIO called these programs EXCEL (Excellence through Customer service Emphasis at Lilbourne) and OLA (One Lilbourne Architecture). The EXCEL and OLA programs followed the company's philosophy of continuous improvement at each process.

The EXCEL program involved the following subsets:

SELL (Sales Environment at Lilbourne Lighting)
A2P (Available to Promise)
MILL (Manufacturing Information at Lilbourne Lighting)
ESS (Effective Scheduling System)
ROLL (Routing Orders at Lilbourne Lighting)
Credit system
BILL (Billing Information at Lilbourne Lighting)

OLA's goal was to provide one face to the market, integrating product lines from different divisions and restructuring existing systems to provide the foundation needed for a $1 billion sales volume. As volume, products, and product customization increased, the present hardware and software foundations became increasingly susceptible to unanticipated problems. A priority was to upgrade the present software and hardware foundations. Microcomputers in the field were already being replaced.

The company had worked toward the client-server model, with the mainframe acting as a central repository and database server while most of the processing is distributed throughout the organization and among market entities. Portions of selected databases would be distributed as well. Extract databases would continue to be used.

The company's CIO and CEO are business heroes, heralded by MIT's Sloan School of Management and by an outstanding state university's business school in the nearby metropolitan area. Friends since high school, the CIO and CEO attended college together. While the CIO worked for a national computer company, the CEO completed an MBA at Harvard University. They have been with the company for 26 of its 44 years and helped the company move from a small, Southern lighting company to a national presence in the commercial/industrial lighting market. Information technology has been used to create a sustained competitive advantage. More than a support function automating clerical and accounting functions, information technology has been used as a marketing weapon. The company has fought the battles to make new technology work, placed microcomputers in agents' offices, networked these microcomputers, and adapted the client-server architecture long before these techniques were touted in business periodicals. The rewards of early adaptation of this new technology have been great. The service provided by these field systems has differentiated products and raised barriers to entry in the market. But the risks were great as well. If a system failed, the company could lose business, not just suffer the annoyance of a late report.

THE OBSERVATION WEEK

The risk factor for the manufacturing CIO was not that experienced by the insurance or university CIO (i.e., the political riskiness of the new position itself). He was well established in the organization. Rather, his risk was in the early adapter strategy the manufacturing company had pursued. Just as information technology is used to gain business, it can also lose business. The CIO role in a company such as this one is pivotal. One day's events during the observation week demonstrate that point clearly and serve as a microcosm for the environment in which the manufacturing CIO operated.

Returning from a three week international business trip, the CIO had been told by the Senior VP of Marketing that the same systems which had provided a competitive advantage in the market place were experiencing so many problems that the effect was backfiring. A Dothan, Alabama, agent had already switched to another supplier out of frustration with system failures. The West coast, especially Los Angeles, had also experienced failures. In fact, the Distribution Manager had encouraged distribution centers and warehouses to use facsimile machines to deliver orders and shipping verifications instead of using the order processing system that was in place. A prominent Los Angeles agent, a former company executive and a Harvard MBA, had written the CEO a long letter detailing the problems he had experienced and his proposed solutions. The CIO agreed with the problems but thought the solutions would cause a loss of data integrity.

At 8:30 A.M., the CIO went to the conference room adjacent to his office and wrote on the board with a red marker: "Meeting Topic: Improving Performance." He filled his coffee cup and began to pace impatiently, eager for the 8:45 A.M. meeting to begin. Key I&MS staff members, some three levels away from him in the formal structure of the I&MS organization, were to attend. The CIO began the meeting by pointing to the topic on the board. "We're here to identify measures we can take immediately to improve performance. We have already gained approval to expand mainframe capacity, increasing the number of access channels. This upgrade will be effective in 30 days." He looked around the room, examining each familiar face, gauging the impact of this announcement. The VP of I&MS had not yet arrived.   He continued, "I have not been involved in day-to-day operations. Now, I'll be looking at daily performance measures. During the Seniors meeting yesterday, I was told that a distributor in Dothan, Alabama, had switched to another supplier because of the downtime experienced. The Senior VP of Marketing told me that the distribution managers who faxed orders to agents and shipping instructions to warehouses were heroes! They should be given medals for entrepreneurship! At least they were responding when the system wasn't working." He paused, waiting for this accusation to sink in, then lowered his voice: "Senior executives are keeping numbers, logs of problems.   Their numbers may not be correct and we may not agree with them, but the very fact that they feel the need to keep numbers is a bad indication. They are saying that we are losing business because we can't keep our systems up." There was no sound in the room. He had their attention.   He continued, "Our problems are very visible. The business depends on our performance. We know that the long-term solution is distributed database management using the client-server model. Then we don't have the same mainframe access problems. But in the interim, we can do better, much better. We're being compared to our own past performance. We're not here to throw blame on anyone, but rather to identify what I'll term *responsiveness problems* which we can control."

The CIO cited an example. A warehouse microcomputer failed to receive its update for SOS (Stock Order System). The CIO asserted that this should never happen. I&MS should be following procedures to monitor transmissions and, he thundered, "respond to a failure like a parent responds to an electrical failure when he has a baby on a iron lung. But maybe kids are like customers. Expendable. Power failure. Throw them away. Have another. File a malfunction report in triplicate."

The manager of the customer support function spoke up: "We've had so many calls lately, more than we can handle. Instead of calling for help, yelling that we have an emergency because we have so many people on hold or call back, we have just become tolerant of customers having to wait to talk to us. We've just become tolerant of all the lines being busy—what we don't get to today, we'll get to tomorrow. We may need some help until some of the problems causing calls are resolved, but we can get our attitudes about problem calls straightened out." The CIO nodded, "Good," and looked around the room for further discussion. "What mainframe performance measures are we reacting to?" Since the Data Processing Director position was open, he looked to the Operations Manager, who had been on the job only a few weeks.

The Operations Manager identified a weekly report. The CIO expanded on the iron lung analogy. "You mean the kid has been dead for a week before you know it?" The Operations Manager admitted that he was really responding to customer complaints. "You mean you're reacting to the kid screaming. We should know the power went out before he does. I want you to identify your pulse points, the places to monitor so that problems can be intercepted. Then use measures of these pulse points as a basis for action," the CIO stated.

The VP of I&MS arrived, and slumped down in his chair. He looked tired. The CIO reviewed the main points made thus far. Then he listed on the board some pulse points or some areas where the group should devote continuous attention. The VP of I&MS quickly became the only participant in the discussion. Others answered only when directly addressed, and then with some hesitation. The VP pointed out that the connect problem was a Netware problem. He complained that Novell was mainly a marketing company and provided little technical assistance. The CIO responded that systems software could be written to compensate for this problem with Netware: "Can you think of a better use of that time? When the connect is not made, we suffer in the market." The VP responded that he would get back to the CIO on this assignment after talking with the systems programmers. Systems programmers were currently assigned to other projects, and a shift in assignments would have to occur. The CIO nodded. He added "shorter connect time" to the action list on the board. Identifying pulse points to measure and monitor in each area was already on the action list.

Then he looked up and asked quietly, "Where is the SOS machine located now? Who sits beside it to know when modem lights are not blinking, when the screen delivers an error message?" The VP responded that it was currently in a room by itself because of vacation time granted. The CIO asked why it was not put in the middle of the room where the staff supporting SOS worked. The VP responded that there was no room for the machine in the office. The CIO bellowed, "Put it in the middle of the room where the coffee pot is because that was what was in the middle of the room this morning!" Then he said more quietly, "What's important here? Hire someone to stand by it and scream for help when lights quit blinking if that's what it takes. I want a person monitoring that system constantly before the sun sets today." He called his administrative assistant and asked her to reschedule an applicant interview. This meeting was lasting longer than he anticipated.

After a short coffee break, he reiterated, "We must take very visible and effective action now. For us, the customer—the agent, the distributor, the warehouse—is our baby on an iron lung. Two items remain on the agenda: eliminating the faxing of orders now and formulating a plan to present our systems to a major new opportunity for business. So, why are our customers in the fax business anyway?" The VP, who had been recruited from a copy machine company, responded. One of his strong points was considered to be his technical competence. He explained that when the mainframe is down or there is partial availability, orders cannot be processed. Product availability must be confirmed and inventory allocated to process the orders. This requires the mainframe's inventory database. Although orders may be entered by distributors (DIAL-L or the DIstributor Access to Lilbourne Lighting) and warehouses (SOS+), all orders must be processed through the agent (ACE+), who is on-line with the mainframe. If the mainframe is not available to the agent, the order is not processed and no bill of lading is created for the distribution center or warehouse to ship the product. Distribution centers faxed copies of the order to the warehouse so that the warehouse could use the paper order to assemble and then ship the order. The CIO listened patiently and then added, "So orders are shipped from inventory which may have been allocated to another customer and inventory is depleted without changing the inventory database and thus the manufacturing schedule. We can improve mainframe performance, but in the interim why not install printers at distribution centers and warehouses having the most problems so that when the order processing system is down, the order can still be entered and printed at the appropriate locations? Then that printout can be used to keep trucks moving. Problems will result, but the order entry will be complete and problems quickly identified." The CIO turned to the Field Systems Manager and asked, "When can this be done?" The manager discussed tasks with another manager and replied that the printers could be working in three days. The CIO added "Printers working Tuesday" to the action list. He then changed the subject of the meeting.

"During the meeting today we're looking at both sides of the coin. At the same time that our systems are causing critical problems, we are proposing them as the key factor in our marketing strategy for a major new opportunity. We have a major customer who is currently doing $12 million in sales with us annually. They have decided to use one source for lighting, which will mean $30 to $40 million in business, with the prospect of this amount increasing to $100 million. They've looked at all the major lighting companies and settled on two, one of which is our company. Despite the performance problems experienced lately, the Seniors all agreed yesterday that our systems are our main competitive advantage in this situation. We can install the distributor system (DIAL-L) at the customer site and let the customer enter orders, confirm orders, and check order status. The Seniors agreed that this service and quick turnaround on orders is what we can do that our major competitor can't do. So I want you to leave with things in perspective. Our systems aren't bad, they're critical. Thus, it's urgent to fix failures. Expectations of our systems' performance must be lived up to on a second-by-second basis. And we must figure out how to do this without being here 24 hours a day."

The CIO then asked a few staff members to remain for planning the details of the customer presentation. He summarized the situation. The themes for the presentation were convenience and speed. The customer had a bad experience with Electronic Data Interchange (EDI): "We need to indicate our expertise in this area and willingness to help. We also need to promote our training and support function." The group decided to prototype a DIAL-L system, customizing screens with the customer's name and product nomenclature. The Training Manager took responsibility for providing a slide presentation to be used by the CIO during his presentation to the customer. The meeting was over at 11:15 A.M. The CIO was scheduled to interview a candidate for a microcomputer engineering position next.

Speaking to the applicant, the CIO explained why the applicant had gone through six interviews already: "We're leery of divorces so we don't get married too quickly." He explained that the lighting market is not growing, so the company must take a competitor's business if it is to grow: "Information systems are one of our key competencies." He also discussed the intelligent building market and the new residential decorative lighting market. The applicant had lost his job at a local high-technology company which implemented a sudden reduction in force just two weeks after the applicant had been hired. The CIO explained that LL's last major reduction in force occurred in the 1974 construction downturn but that the way to address stability in any environment was to address one's own productivity and work toward a continuum of improvement. He cited the quotation "I love you more today than yesterday but not as much as tomorrow" as an example of how a person's value to a company should continue to increase. He indicated that his opinion of the cause for the high-technology company's failure was top management's apathy, being satisfied with the status quo or resting on their laurels.

At 12:15 P.M., the CIO was scheduled for a lunch meeting with the VP of the Controls Division. They sat at the table called "Charlie's [CIO's] office" by the waitress. The VP placed his list of items to discuss, written neatly on a "stick-on" note card, beside his napkin and methodically began to discuss each item in some detail. He noted follow-up items beside each topic. He brought an advertising brochure with him, and the two worked on improving its wording and layout. He also relayed his concerns about the contract for an intelligent building network protocol, indicating serious omissions in the information provided by the vendor—areas in which surprises might occur. The VP of

Controls had previously served as the VP of Management Services, with responsibility for field systems before the reorganization. Now he had been given the opportunity to grow a business, using the expertise acquired in the LightLink implementation. His college ring indicated that he had attended the same university as the CEO and CIO.

The CIO assured the VP that he would discuss his contract concerns with the CEO of the supplier. They had become friends working together on the Technical Committee of the Intelligent Building Institute. The CIO served as Chairman of this committee.

The CIO returned to his office for a 2:10 P.M. interview with the applicant for Director of Data Processing. This applicant had also been separated from the same high-technology company as the microcomputer engineering applicant. He had been with the company for 18 months as the Technical Services Manager. Prior to this experience, he had been with the same company for 20 years. In his last position there, he had been responsible for operations and technical services. After his children left home, he and his wife decided to look for a challenge and a change. He had not regretted the move.

The CIO confided in the applicant that he was very concerned about the I&MS group. Returning to work after attending the annual Executive Meeting in Greece and visiting some agents in Egypt, he was confronted with a series of crises. He also confided that he had hoped to retire in three years. After investing 26 years in the organization, he wanted to be sure the competitive advantage provided by information technology would be sustained and not backfire. He asked the applicant if the VP of I& MS had told him about the turnover problem among the technical staff. The applicant nodded but seemed interested in hearing the CIO's reasons. The CIO continued, "A mutual decision was reached. The Data Processing Director decided that he was not a good fit for the pressures accompanying a $1 billion sales volume, which is where we're heading. He was a well-liked member of the company family. Some of our technical people made the same decision."

The applicant responded that the VP had given him two goals for the open position: (1) rebuild operations and (2) stabilize technical services. The CIO hastened to add a third goal: provide a high level of customer service. "We're about lighting, not about computers." He provided an example to illustrate his point. "If you ask a farmer what their critical task is, they don't say, 'ride a tractor.' No, they say, 'raise corn.' Our customers are our agents, distributors, engineers who specify our product, warehouses which carry our product, and contractors who install the product. If you were hired, we'd make a lighting businessperson out of you first and a computer person second—send you to school on lighting, teach you to calculate the appropriate lighting for a room, be sure you understand our products and how our customers work on a day-to-day basis." The applicant nodded and replied: "I've been to the library to read what I could find about Lilbourne Lighting. I read the article where you said that we had to know the business, not run around like 'three headed yo-yos serving the data processing god.'" The applicant laughed. The CIO nodded, then changed the subject to a discussion of the company's future IT architecture.

At 2:45 P.M., the CIO met with the CEO. The CIO was scheduled to deliver a speech before the parent company's Board of Directors Saturday morning. He previewed the speech for the CEO. The topic was the Management, Information, and Electronics Services (MIES) division. The CIO's administrative assistant also attended the meeting so that changes could be noted and brought to closure. They had worked together for 20 years; she was a master of detail and organization. The presentation emphasized a theme begun by the company founder in the 1950s. This philosophy and the division itself were symbolized by the picture of a runner wearing the number 421: four groups to one goal, "Making Lilbourne Lighting easy to do business with." The CEO listened closely, and many details were changed. He liked the presentation but seemed concerned. After the preview, the CIO told him that he would meet with the Senior VP of Marketing and Sales this afternoon concerning their discussion yesterday. He also told him that he thought the staff meeting this morning had been productive and watched his friend's face carefully. The CEO nodded and simply responded, "Good."

From 4:00 to 5:00 P.M., the CIO met with the Senior Vice Presidents of Marketing and Sales. The CIO began the meeting by saying that the problems being experienced were his fault. The mainframe is "out of gas." The VP of I&MS, who was present at the meeting, knew this but understood that the plan was for distributed processing and didn't want to spend any more money on mainframes. Also, I&MA had thought that an upgrade would be much more expensive than the deal negotiated yesterday. The upgrade was available and would be installed in 30 days. Response time would improve and less downtime would be experienced with order processing. The Senior VP of Sales responded enthusiastically, "Boy, Charlie, that's great. Thirty days you say," and made a note in his calendar. "You know, until we talked last night, I had no idea how important these phone lines are, too." He turned to the Senior VP of Sales, "Charlie was telling me that if a bird happens to, uh, go to the john on a line somewhere, an agent could be hung up for hours, not able to connect." They all laughed. The CIO responded, "I want ya'll to understand where we're headed," and began to draw a picture of where distributed databases and dedicated lines were planned.

As he drew, the VP of I&MS spoke up: "I want you guys to know that we're working on one cause of terminals hanging up." He explained a problem with locked records and the work now being done to correct the problem. The two Senior VPs and the Distribution Manager, who had come with them, nodded politely and stared ahead. The CIO slapped the picture drawn on the board and pointed to dedicated lines between key distribution centers, and warehouses, agents and to distributed database sites. Very little detail was given. He moved on quickly: "But during this 30 days we're not going to be sitting on our hands. The work which is improving our systems for the future—but is also using mainframe capacity—has been halted as of today. This should cause a noticeable improvement in response time." The Senior VP of Marketing interrupted, "Charlie, are you sure that's been done? I was told," and he turned to look at the VP of I&MS, "that this had been done two weeks ago but I haven't noticed any difference. In fact, some of my sources tell me this activity is still going on." There was a heavy silence. The CIO did not respond. The VP of I&MS responded, "I've put the word out. No more changes. I'll follow up on that and make sure." The CIO nodded.

Then the CIO looked up and smiled brightly. "Now we've got to stop building Towers of Babylon with fax machines! We can't keep the mainframe from ever going down or prevent all connect problems and so on. But we can give distributors and agents who are going down the ability to print entered but unconfirmed orders when problems occur. We'll be able to print order entries on the West Coast, where we've had the most problems, this Tuesday. I understand the Los Angeles Distribution Center should be our first target." The VP of Marketing was very interested. The VP of Sales nodded briskly. The CIO explained that the use of printers would be enhanced over time, allowing customers to select ranges of orders to print or just one order. But the printout in a rough, usable form would be available Tuesday. The mood of the meeting shifted as the CIO's responsiveness to the complaints received yesterday became evident. The Senior VP of Sales said, "Charlie, this is great. Appreciate it," and stood up to leave. The Senior VP of Marketing shook hands with the CIO, "We can live with this Charlie. Thanks."

The VP of I&MS stayed over to tell the CIO that the systems program to bypass connect problems could be ready in two weeks if the systems programmer did nothing else. The CIO responded, "Can you think of a better use of this resource now? Two weeks, then." He added, "I'm for hiring the applicant for the Data Processing Director job." They discussed the offer to be made.

That evening, the CIO worked two hours at home. Some of his major insights into the business had occurred sitting in his basement office. The enterprise model which revealed the central position of the agent and the need to place systems with the agents first had been developed in his basement office using a personal computer graphics package. That evening, he continued his work on a proposal for company-wide pricing policies and procedures.

This one day's events depicts vividly the risks and rewards of using information technology to compete. Clearly, the risks are greatly reduced by a CIO who can communicate with functional areas, the IT unit, and other executives, by a CIO who knows the business and has technical competence. This CIO understood the power of words to shape his audience's perception of the world, using analogies, stories, and graphics skillfully and avoiding technical jargon. Even acronyms made sense. He commented that he had become a "scribe" for the Senior Seven, always capturing major decisions in writing to make sure they "hold water." Clearly, the technical, "DP Manager" approach taken by his second in command, the VP of I&MS, had been less effective. The CIO was not an enhancement in this environment. The role was essential for the strategy pursued. An overview of other observation days follows.

The first day began with the CIO completing work on a presentation to be delivered at MIT and then reviewing desk work with his administrative assistant in her office. A meeting with the IT group followed, during which screens for an agent entry program were discussed. A database clean-up project and deadlines for various projects were also discussed. Then the group concentrated on GUIDE, their Graphical User Interface Data Environment. Schedules, objectives, and preparations for a joint application development session were reviewed. The CIO then passed on news from the latest Seniors meeting. His administrative assistant interrupted the meeting so that he could take a call from the CEO. Following the meeting, he began a conference call with a protocol vendor for intelligent buildings.

The second day, the CIO reported a phone call at home from a New York agent. The call had lasted over one and a half hours. He completed incoming desk work, revised a section of the new pricing policy, wrote to the Department of Energy regarding a document he had read on the greenhouse effect and the lighting industry, received a call from the head of the IS program at a local university, and then drove to the airport for the trip to Boston. He carried desk work and a portable PC with him. Arriving at the hotel, he received fax mail and met an applicant for the Director of MIS position. Following the interview, he joined a prominent MIT researcher for dinner. During dinner, he initiated a detailed discussion on Executive Support System products and vendors. As a result, the researcher promised to make several vendor and industry introductions. Returning to the hotel, he read another Department of Energy correspondence on the warming effect and dictated his response via voice mail to his office. He also dictated a summary of the conference call held yesterday to be issued in the form of a letter.

During the third day, he attended a strategy presentation at MIT conducted by Dr. Michael Scott-Morton and then gave a presentation for Dr. Jack Rockart's (MIT professor and renowned information technology researcher) information technology seminar. Following this seminar, he attended a luncheon during which a Nobel prize winner in economics spoke on the role of government regulation. He then traveled to Chicago, where he was scheduled to review an acquisition or joint venture proposal. During the flight, he studied new material on the proposal. He joined the President of the Chicago company for dinner that evening. While traveling, he participated in 14 phone calls. After dinner, he dictated his impressions of the meeting and the new material reviewed during travel. This letter was to be sent to other senior executives.

The full day spent at the Chicago company studying the product and company was not used since the observer was not present at these confidential meetings. This day of the week was made up five weeks later. The next morning, the CIO attended two meetings at corporate headquarters. As he walked into the building, he asked the CEO's secretary about her husband's health and picked up a paper cup he spotted on the grass.

The first meeting was with Finance and a product division. The status of an expansion and expenditure timing was discussed. The second meeting was a systems review meeting in the executive conference room. The system was to provide an answer to the question, "Can I promise this product to this customer by a certain date?" The decision was made to use established lead times unless an opportunity based on lead time presented itself. The CEO asserted that the system's most powerful capability was to look at how that commitment to a new opportunity based on a special lead time would affect other orders. Would the company lose business by taking what appeared to be an opportunity? One Senior VP said that the most difficult problem was resolving the policy problems, which would enable the system to make many decisions. The CIO answered that the opportunity is to let the customer know that he or she is talking to a group who listens; the customer is not being handled "like cattle." The CEO asked the CIO to stay over after the meeting to discuss the Chicago visit.

Following this meeting with the CEO, the CIO met the VP of a product division for lunch. They reviewed resumes and new government codes for products, and the CIO signed a personnel notice for posting. He made a phone call from his cellular phone at the table to reschedule an interview. Returning to the office, he handled priority desk work with his administrative assistant in her office, interviewed a programmer/analyst candidate, and then talked with the Vice President of I&MS until 7 P.M.

The CIO told me that his job required stamina first and foremost. He also believed that an effective CIO cannot be a "baseball player" moving from team to team: CIOs must know the business and the people in that business.

Chronology Record

A quantitative analysis of the CIO's week shows that he spent 19% of his time on desk work (Appendix A.1), with each session lasting about 45 minutes. Like the university CIO who worked at home and averaged 42-minute desk work sessions, the CIO's uninterrupted work at home increased the average length of desk work sessions. Twenty-three percent of his desk work was performed at home compared to 21% for the university CIO (Appendix A.2). While the university CIO's propensity for work at home seemed to be a preference derived from his academic background, the manufacturing CIO's fast-paced day made uninterrupted reflection and composition very difficult, even with a highly capable administrative assistant who screened his mail and calls. Much of the desk work was handled by the administrative assistant. He visited her office for a review of desk work, skimming where necessary and signing where necessary. Ninety-six percent of desk work was performed in locations other than his office, atypical of other CIOs observed. Thirty-four percent was in subordinate's office, 30% was away from the organization while traveling or having a business lunch, and 9% in the conference room, mostly after meetings. What would normally be considered desk work sessions occurred at home and while traveling. The CIO commented that travel time often allowed him catch up time for desk work. He travelled with a portable microcomputer and received/sent fax mail at each stop.

Twelve percent of the CIO's time was spent on telephone calls (Appendix A.1). The length of his phone calls was twice the average of six minutes. His phone calls often resembled unscheduled meetings. Because his administrative assistant handled many phone calls for him, getting his response to less complex questions and conveying it to the caller, the calls he took tended to require discussion.

Scheduled meetings consumed 56% of his total time and unscheduled meetings consumed 12%. He was in meetings over two thirds of his time. He did not "wander about" or tour during the observation week, except on two occasions and then briefly.

Verbal Contacts

Eighty-one percent of the CIO's total time was spent in verbal contact mediums. Of this verbal contact time, 69% was in scheduled meetings with phone calls and unscheduled meetings consuming 15% each (Appendix A.2). Fifty-seven percent of scheduled meetings had more than four people, including the CIO. Thirty-seven percent of the scheduled meetings were one-on-one. The manufacturing CIO's meetings tended to have more participants than other CIOs observed. Fewer of his contacts and less of his contact time was with subordinates. More time was spent with external peers and trade organizations, independents, and others. He reported directly to the CEO and had only five peers. His interaction with internal peers may have been less because there were fewer of them than at the insurance company, for example, where there were 13 senior vice presidents.

According to this CIO, one of the reasons for maintaining and nourishing contacts with academic "trade organizations" was that these contacts enhanced his ability to recruit. The CIO interviewed applicants for all information technology positions, including programmers. He considered the selection process to be critical, a strategic decision. Although his contact with Mintzberg's "Director" or superior category was close to the average, it was with only one person. Clearly, the CIO and CEO had easy, informal access to each other.

The manufacturing CIO initiated a smaller percentage of verbal contacts (34% compared to 65, 49, 45, and 40% for other CIOs). More than half (52%) of contacts were initiated by the opposite party. Most of the contacts took place in the conference room adjacent to the CIO's office. The layout of his work area, which was in the IT building rather than corporate offices, is helpful for understanding his verbal contacts as well as his desk work. The manufacturing CIO conducted most scheduled meetings in a conference room adjoining his office, separated from his office by a coffee or refreshment area. This area was behind his desk or accessed by the "back door" to his office. In front of his desk, which he seldom used, were visitor's chairs and behind these, near the front door of the office, was a seating arrangement with of a sofa, two chairs, and a coffee table. Outside the front door to his office was his administrative assistant's office, which had two side chairs. Access to the front door of the CIO's office was through the administrative assistant's office. She was positioned and functioned as the gatekeeper.

The CIO conducted most scheduled meetings in the adjoining conference room. For two meetings, he traveled less than five minutes to conference rooms at the corporate office. He traveled away from the organization for one and a half days of the five-day observation. He conducted one interview in a hotel lobby. Furthermore, he conducted working lunch meetings, complete with cellular phone, at a local restaurant. He used the seating arrangement in his office for applicant interviews and his desk area for private phone calls, such as those with the CEO. His desk area functioned mainly as a holding area for his home office. He never held a meeting from behind his imposing desk. Instead, he chose the conference room and seating arrangement for more open exchange.

The largest single-purpose category reflects this exchange. Thirty-seven percent of contact time was spent in review, a session in which information is given and received. The percent of time spent on Mintzberg's strategy purpose was fairly typical (25%).

Incoming Mail

Incoming mail (Appendix A.3) was mostly in the form of memos (51%). This CIO did not study mail. Mail which might have required study versus read or skim was often presented to the CIO verbally by his administrative assistant or the manager who wrote the piece. These reviews facilitated rapid review of incoming mail. Forty-eight percent of the incoming mail was from subordinates and 8% was from internal peers. The remaining 36% was from external sources.

The mail was screened, except for periodicals. The CIO wanted all those forwarded to him and reviewed them at home. Periodicals thus constituted a fairly higher percent of incoming mail (20%); but two other CIOs received even more periodicals, the government agency CIO and the utility CIO. These two CIOs also tracked news events which would influence the vendor or political environment. The manufacturing CIO subscribed to IT periodicals and lighting industry periodicals.

On average, the 355 pieces of incoming mail for the five CIOs were 35% requests or decisional and 65% information. The incoming mail for the manufacturing CIO was 54% requests and 46% informational. Almost half of his incoming mail was authority requests, or requests which required his approval and/or signature. Because the administrative assistant and CIO had worked together for over 20 years, she could select mail he needed to see effectively and brief him on the rest.

Outgoing Mail

The manufacturing CIO initiated 92% of his outgoing mail instead of responding to incoming mail. He dictated the draft of most letters from notes. He was able to call into the office while traveling or at home and dictate letters. He then edited the printed draft. Seventy-eight percent of his outgoing mail targets were either the CEO or his peers among the Senior Seven.

The topic of these letters was a new pricing policy for the company's products. At present, each division had its own pricing policies. These different policies were an obstacle to the company's strategy to present "one face to the market" or to provide a package of lighting products meeting all the needs of the building specifier. Furthermore, work on an electronic catalog with pricing provided at one source was becoming entangled in conflicting policies. Another topic was an explanation of OLA+ (One Lilbourne Architecture plus enhancements) or the information technology architecture for the company.

Activity Durations

The manufacturing CIO's activities tended to be longer than other CIOs observed (Appendix C). The VP of I&MS handled many of the operational details. Furthermore, the administrative assistant handled many matters which could have been handled through a brief contact.

Interaction Analysis

Although all five CIOs spent more than half of their time outside the information technology unit (Appendix H.1), the manufacturing CIO spent the highest percentage (71%). While his percent of contacts and percent of contact time with functional areas was close to the average, his percent of contacts and contact time with external participants was double the average. External verbal contacts included a full day at MIT, applicants for openings in the MIES division, contacts with an intelligent building trade group, and the president of a company developing a protocol for intelligent buildings.

Only 9% of the mail was received from or targeted for the information technology group only (Appendix D.1). Ninety-one percent involved external, functional, or mixed groups. An example of mixed mail was the pricing policy, which was targeted to functional areas and information technology unit members.

Responsibility Analysis

Verbal Contacts

Three responsibilities (Appendix E) consumed 78% of the manufacturing CIO's verbal contact time:

Strategic planning	36%
Consulting, present problems	24%
Coordination of three groups:	
IT, external, internal	18%

Clearly, the CIO was a bridge between the IT group and other entities because he could see the problem from a business, not merely a technical, perspective.

Desk Work

Forty-five percent of desk work was categorized under the responsibility of approval or acceptance of an acquisition or expense. Forty-three percent of desk work was oriented toward the long term considerations of strategic planning; policies, procedures, guidelines; and environmental scanning. Desk work devoted to other general managerial work was at the lowest for the five CIOs.

Verbal Contacts and Desk Work

On an occurrence basis for all desk work and contacts (Appendix E.3), approval or acceptance of expenditures is still the major responsibility (26%). Strategic planning was the responsibility for 20% of occurrences. Coordination of the three groups (16%) ranked third.

Roles Analysis

Verbal Contacts

Although the resource allocator role was required for 45% of all verbal contacts (Appendix F), this role consumed only 23% of all contact time. On an occurrence and time basis, the three dominant roles were resource allocator, monitor, and disturbance handler.

While only 29% of verbal contacts time was informational, these contacts consumed 40% of contact time. Decisional roles consumed 67% of contact time, and the interpersonal role of figurehead consumed 4%. With verbal contacts, the liaison rather than leader role was dominant, as it was with all CIOs.

Scheduled meetings were the medium for 41% of the monitoring activity, with the CIO listening to updates and asking questions. Unscheduled meetings required the disturbance-handler role 32% of the time. Forty-five percent of unscheduled meetings were resource allocation requests. Similarly, 57% of phone calls were resource allocation requests. Disturbance handling, while only 17% of phone call occurrences, consumed the highest amount of phone time (35%).

Desk Work

Almost half of the mail required the resource allocator role. Twenty-three percent called for the monitor role and 15% the entrepreneur. As would be expected, only a small percentage of mail required disturbance handling. Thirty percent of desk work was informational and 70% decisional. The resource allocator role was called for mainly for incoming rather than outgoing desk work. Outgoing mail was primarily entrepreneurial (50%) with the spokesman role accounting for 25% of occurrences. Desk work required the liaison role 91% of the time.

Verbal Contacts and Desk Work

On an occurrence basis for all contacts and desk work, 47% of the manufacturing CIO's occurrences of mail and verbal contacts required the role of resource allocator. Twenty one percent was monitoring and 11% disturbance handling. These three roles—resource allocator, monitor, disturbance handler—accounted for almost 80% of all occurrences of mail and contacts. Sixty-eight percent of all occurrences were decisional roles, 29% informational and 2% the interpersonal role of figurehead.

7

The Insurance Company CIO

BACKGROUND

Company

Begun in 1955 by the current CEO's uncle as a supplemental cancer expense insurer, United States Insurers (USI; an alias) has expanded its product line to eight insurance products and is exploring additional products, some of which are outside the insurance industry. However, the influence of the founder and the founding mission remains strong. The company continues to participate in niche markets, seeking specialty products where competition is less intense. Furthermore, the company strives to differentiate its product by the quality of service provided to claimants and sales agents. A three-day turnaround is the goal for servicing every claim.

A conservative company, USI has not invested in junk bonds but invests in highly liquid assets with predictable cash flows. According to the executive responsible for investments, "Consistent, predictable, above-average growth is the number one goal" of his company. Stock is publicly traded on the New York Stock Exchange and Tokyo Stock Exchange.

Despite this conservative investment approach, marketing and distribution methods are innovative. In fact, *Forbes* magazine recently named this insurer the "most innovative insurance company" of the year. USI Officers recently testified to the Congress about their experience in penetrating the Japanese market. The Japan branch now accounts for more than 75% of the company's earnings. Revenues for the past three years have exceeded one-half billion dollars. Return on equity has averaged 19%.

Cluster selling, or selling to employees of an organization through payroll deductions, has proved to be an efficient and effective strategy in Japan. There, companies may legally act as the agent, selling the insurance, making payroll deductions, and earning a commission. Thus, cluster selling in Japan is known as a corporate agency system. Cluster selling differs from group insurance in that sales are made and policies are issued to the individuals (rather than the company) insured. However, sales exposure is maximized by being able to make group presentations.

Cluster selling also leverages the high quality of USI's claimant service, increasing the persistency or continued enrollment of policyholders. With a tangible good such as a car, the car's continued performance allows the buyer to evaluate on an ongoing basis his or her investment, notes the 1989 annual report. With an intangible product such as specialty health insurance products, the buyer is dealing with intangibles such as "security, stability, and peace of mind." Thus, the prompt, courteous, caring service provided to one claimant acts as an ongoing assurance to others in the same workplace that the purchase is a good one. The service mindset must therefore permeate all those with whom the policyholder and agent interact. According to USI's 1989 annual report,

Customer evaluation of an intangible product like insurance is different. The only time a person evaluates the decision to purchase is when the policy is needed, but that need may not arise for 5 or 10 years or even longer. Therefore, it is important to reinforce the customer's purchasing decision every time he or she comes in contact with the Company. [USI] does this by striving to provide the absolute best customer service. We believe this begins by motivating all employees in the Home Office to understand and commit themselves to service.

Until the present decade, superior service was more a policy than a requirement for competition.

A family feeling has been cultivated among USI employees, agents, and policyholders. Family relationships dominate executive management. The current CEO is the nephew of the former CEO and was previously the Deputy CEO. He has worked for the company since his teens and majored in risk and insurance management at a state university. His father is the brother of the founder and is among the principal founders of the company. His father now serves as Vice Chairman of the Board. The career path of three of these four top executives has been in sales, and the other has been in finance. The First Senior Vice President, to who the CIO reports, has also worked for the company since his teens and graduated from the same state university as the CEO. His career path has also been in sales. Among the team of 17 executive management and senior vice presidents, 12 have been with the company for 10 years or longer. All but one of the senior vice presidents has been with the company for five years or more, and that one is the medical doctor who serves on the Board and as the Medical Director. The CIO or Senior Vice President of the Information Systems Division has been associated with the company for five years, so he is a newcomer among other senior managers.

The top management group is a tight-knit group with long-standing personal as well as professional relationships. A company newspaper and magazine encourages all employees to participate in company-sponsored activities and keeps employees informed of the professional and personal achievements of their coworkers. The company founder and his wife are sometimes referred to as "Mr. Joe" and "Miss Ellen" (aliases used) in these publications. Being a sales associate is often a family affair. The company newsletters often note that a son or daughter has also joined the company as a sales associate.

Since the early 1980s, the comfort of this family company has been disrupted by a changing environment. Health care costs have risen dramatically. Providing coverage at affordable costs has become more difficult for both traditional and niche market insurers. As the population ages and health care costs increase, Medicare is being supplemented with "Medigap" products. These products provide coverage for items not covered by Medicare and/or cover the difference in actual costs and the cost paid for by Medicare. Another critical demographic shift during the 1980s was in income distribution. According to the company's *Financial Analysts' Briefing*,

Ten years ago our society was predominantly middle class, and insurance products were geared to that large market. Today, the picture is radically different. Income distribution in the U.S. shifted to the lower and higher income groups, resulting in a drastically reduced middle class. Our old cancer plan [pre-1984] was directed primarily to the middle class; the new family of cancer plans addresses the entire marketplace.

Reducing costs to provide coverage has been necessary. Consequently, downsizing and restructuring have resulted.

A new business strategy was formulated to respond to growing competitiveness and demographic shifts. This strategy, while broadening the product base, was implemented with the company's commitment to remain the "dominant force in all the markets we serve" (*Financial Analysts' Briefing*). At the heart of the new strategy was Computer Services, now know as the Information Systems Division (ISD).

According to the current CEO, who played a major role in this new strategy, the move from a one-product company to a "broader-based supplemental health insurance provider" was planned in three phases. In the first phase, existing policies were reviewed from the perspective of policy holders, sales associates, and company profitability. As a result of this review, new cancer policies were "age banded," with different rates for different age groups. The average age of policy holders had increased, causing the risk of claims to increase. Instead of increasing all premiums, age banding was implemented. The company lost many sales associates with this change.

In the second phase of this new strategy, an infrastructure to support product growth was implemented, with new administrative and computer systems. This infrastructure has culminated in a state-of-the-art new Data Center, which "now provides computer services so good that the Company's business can be planned without regard to computing limitations," says the current CIO, the Senior VP of the Information Systems Division (ISD), in a recent company newsletter. Major new systems were installed to enhance the speed and quality of customer service. This second phase coincides with the time the present CIO and previous CIO joined the company.

Both had experience with the same insurance company prior to joining USI. One indicant of the importance of information systems planning is that the previous CIO served as chairman of the company's operating committee, a committee with major responsibility for the company's strategy.

With the new administrative and information systems infrastructure in place, the company began to broaden its product base and launched the third phase. A new logo was adopted for the insurance company, the holding company's principal subsidiary, in an effort to improve name recognition. In addition to this new product base, the ISD provided systems support for the decentralization of administrative functions by sales regions and for further automation of the policy assembly process.

ISD is at the core of the company's effort to provide profitable insurance for specialty products across all income distributions and to provide superior service. Nevertheless, information systems remains a technical area within the company, not a career path to top management. Among the 13 senior vice presidents, only two (Senior VP of ISD and Senior VP U.S./Japan) have an information systems background. However, the Senior VP of Administration is an avid personal computer user both at home and work, as are many members of the Finance Department in which local area networks were implemented in the mid-1980s. The CIO uses a personal computer as a terminal for electronic mail. However, the ISD remains a "mainframe shop" requiring specialization and thus some isolation.

Information Systems Division (ISD)

A recent restructuring of the ISD has reduced the number of vice presidents in the division and further isolated programming staff from user contact. Outside consultants were hired to recommend a new structure. The purpose of this restructuring was to reduce the backlog and ensure that IS resources were assigned to projects with high strategic priority.

At the time of the observation, a Business Systems Analyst group provided the conceptual analysis and design for new systems. Then an Application Development group provided the physical design for the Programming Support group. Theoretically, the programming staff has greater flexibility and could be assigned to priority projects for the organization rather than continuing to work on projects from the functional areas to which they might be assigned. Some users have begun to complain about having to deal with so many different people, however. Communications problems because of two layers of analysts between users and programmers have surfaced. In practice, the criterion of assigning scarce resources remains problematic. While some programmers prefer the new organization in which they have minimal contact with users, others, especially the more recent graduates, report that they are less satisfied, according to the CIO. This reorganization was unsatisfactory to the previous CIO (1985-1988) and was one factor leading to his resignation.

The reporting relationship for the ISD chief was also restructured in the last two years. The previous CIO had reported to the CEO's nephew, the subsidiary's Chief Operating Officer and the holding company's Deputy CEO. The current CIO reports to the First Senior VP of Operations.

The new strategy has been the catalyst for much change in the entire organization, including the ISD. This change has met some resistance. Ironically, this change has been necessary for the company to remain unchanged (i.e., to continue to provide affordable specialty health insurance with superior service, to continue to dominate all markets in which it participates, and to generate earnings at a reasonable, predictable annual growth rate). Essentially, the more the company has changed, the more it has stayed the same in terms of its original mission.

If a change in strategy and, consequently, structure had not been implemented, the company would have been forced to change course, accepting lower or riskier growth and providing less affordable coverage in markets in which the company might cease to dominate. The ISD has had to adjust to this change, as have sales agents and administrative personnel.

Keeping the ISD's overriding goals in the forefront has been one approach of the present CIO to override conflict and resistance to change. He initiated a weekly *Customer Service Newsletter*. In the first issue, he introduced his customer service goal and commitment:

I expect to find and reward ISD employees who are performing exceptional customer service, coach individuals and areas who may have become a bit lax, and pretty much try to make each of us examine the level of customer satisfaction that we provide.

ISD members were asked to consider the specific customers to whom they provide products and "estimate their level of satisfaction." In the second issue, responses to this request, using names, were printed. Commendations have been printed in the newsletter as well as results from a customer service survey.

During the move to the new data center, the CIO sent a newsletter to officers, department heads, and managers, keeping them informed of events:

During the months of March and April, there will be an increased level of activity within the Information Systems Division with regard to our move to the new Data Center. We would like to take the opportunity with this memorandum, and a few others during the next two months, to let you know what's going on. In particular, we would like to tell you why we are moving, how we intend to do it, what the setup and security will be at the new site, and what will be different after we have moved.

In the company newsletter, the CIO explained the change and stated the ISD's goal for the move itself:

The new facility will allow us to put in the additional computer systems the Company needs to continue growing. We hope we'll be able to translate all of this into additional capabilities for our customers at [USI]. Our goal was to make the move with no interruption of service.

The insurance CIO is a consensus builder and a stabilizing force. He is sensitive to the close, long-standing personal and professional relationships among senior vice presidents and is working to become accepted by this group, personally as well as professionally. Although he reads *CIO* magazine, he explained the observer's presence as a study of "what the data processing guy does" instead of "study the chief information officer role" or "study the job of the person in charge of information resources." When questioned about why this introduction was made, he responded that he is still the new kid on the block with the senior management group. He doesn't need to do anything that would intimidate other senior managers. His main concern seems to be building trust after a period of major change. Information technology has assumed a new importance to the organization with the new strategy. The marketing effort is dependent upon computing capacity and flexibility.

The CIO gave me a copy of the position questionnaire he completed for Human Resources. He thought this questionnaire would help me understand his role as he views it. He described the overall purpose of his job as the "supervision, coordination, and responsibility for data processing, new technology, and computer utility services" for the U.S. branch of the insurance subsidiary. He lists six tasks performed on a regular basis, and three on an occasional basis. Tasks performed regularly are (1) management of ISD personnel; (2) preparation of reports, budgets, etc.; (3) coordination of ISD activities; (4) review of new technology; (5) general management meetings; and (6) conferring with non-ISD divisions. Types of tasks performed occasionally are (1) acquisition of companies, (2) initiatives to retain current policyholders, and (3) participation in an industry task force to reengineer a major insurance system.

Within the company, the CIO said that he interacts with subsidiary and holding company executives, ISD staff, vendors, auditors, and consultants. Outside the company, he regularly interacts with vendors and consultants. According to the questionnaire, the CIO manages a capital budget of $6 million and an expense budget of $10 million annually. Nevertheless, he refers final decisions for "expenditures over $10,000" and "long-range ISD direction" to the First Senior Vice President of Operations. In answer to a question regarding his impact on company policy, he indicated that his recommendations concerned "technology, computer system implementation, and hardware selection."

These tasks and interactions would be compared to the week's observation. However, the overall impression of the position which emerges from the questionnaire is that the technical rather than the business aspect of the job is emphasized. It seems that care was taken not to assume too much responsibility, especially in strategic areas. According to the present CIO, the ISD's impact is on "general productivity" not on competitive advantage or increased revenues, even though the new strategy prescribed an expansion of computer services for these reasons.

THE OBSERVATION WEEK

The CIO came in early each morning, allowing himself 30 minutes of quiet time for coffee and desk work. Major items on his agenda for the week were evaluating a new strategic planning initiative sponsored by the CEO, exploring the functions and cost of an image processing system, and coordinating the move to the new data center. Both he and his secretary agreed that the week was as typical "as typical gets," except for the disruption of moving his office on Friday afternoon. He continued to function during the move, however.

The CIO's secretary sorted his mail, eliminating an estimated two thirds of it. Memos and letters were written longhand on pads and word processed by the secretary. Some memos were received and sent through a mainframe-based electronic mail system accessed via a microcomputer. Desk work did not involve the use of a microcomputer otherwise. Air travel time was used for verbal interaction rather than reserved for a travel folder of desk work.

Chronology Record

Desk work consumed only 14% of the CIO's time and verbal interactions consumed 86% of his time (Appendix B.1-B.4). Of the five CIOs studied, the insurance CIO devoted the least amount of time to desk work and telephone calls and the most amount of time to unscheduled meetings and tours. He initiated 65% of his verbal contacts. The insurance CIO was "out and about" in the organization more frequently than other CIOs observed, with 35% of his verbal contacts occurring in the hall or work areas (Appendix B.2).

Verbal Contacts

Most of these verbal contacts in the hall or work areas occurred in the Data Center, where the CIO kept a second office. His primary office is now at headquarters, a few blocks away, but he is scheduled to move to the Data Center within the year. At the Data Center, he frequently toured and dropped in on subordinates. He encouraged informality and openness, calling ISD members by their first names, asking about family members and hobbies. Nevertheless, an ISD meeting attended by all division employees changed mood immediately after the CIO left. People chatted more, interrupted subsequent speakers with jokes and kidding, and laughed frequently. A relaxed "just us" mood prevailed.

The CIO seemed to be bridging two worlds—that of the ISD and senior executive—and working to become accepted by both. With the executive group, his strategy seemed to be to represent himself as a technical person, a data processing guy. He represented himself as technically oriented on his job questionnaire as well, yet he seemed to rely on subordinates for technical decisions and advice. Within the ISD group, the image he projected was that of a senior manager in touch with other senior managers. He brought the technical side to the management group and the management side to the technical group with some deliberateness (thus the problem with fit in both groups). However, both groups were given a direct representation of each other.

Incoming Mail

An analysis of incoming mail (Appendix B.3) shows that 63% of it came from subordinates and only 3% from superiors. Input mail in the form of letters was almost double the average for all CIOs and easily the highest percentage for this form. Memos received constituted 45% of the mail, and this percentage was typical. The attention level given to the mail was 32% skimmed, 50% read, and 18% studied. The percentage of mail studied versus skimmed or read was also above the average. The purpose of the insurance company CIO's incoming mail was 53% requests (29% solicitations and 24% authorizations) and 47% informational. Twenty-four percent of the incoming mail was received through the electronic mail system.

Outgoing Mail

Outgoing mail was in the form of a letter or memo 86% of the time (Appendix B.4). Seventy-three percent was self-initiated as opposed to being a reaction to input. The target of output mail was subordinates (77%), peers (18%), and superiors (5%). The electronic mail system was used for 36% of the output.

Interaction Analysis

A verbal interaction analysis by group membership or area shows that the

CIO's contacts with information technology associates accounted for 64% of verbal contacts but only 44% of contact time (Appendix H.7). Fifty-six percent of contact time was spent with those not in the ISD or with ISD and other groups together. Only 2% of the verbal contact time was with those external to the company.

The insurance and government agency CIO had the highest percentage of total pieces of mail targeted or received from within the information technology group, 58% and 57% respectively (Appendix C.1). Twenty percent of the insurance company CIO's mail was with those external to the environment and 22% with functional areas; thus, 42% of the total pieces of mail represent interactions outside the information technology area. This analysis substantiates the CIO's role in coordinating the three areas and bridging the gap between the ISD and other areas. Clearly, his verbal and nonverbal interactions are in all three areas: functional, environment or external, and information technology.

Activity Duration

The duration of this CIO's activities tended to be briefer than the other CIO's (Appendix B.1). Eighty-nine percent of his activities lasted 15 minutes or less. The fact that this CIO initiated a higher percentage of his contacts in locations other than his office contributed to the brevity of many contacts. His unscheduled meetings percentage was also double the average for other CIOs.

Responsibility Analysis

Each piece of mail and each verbal contact was coded by eight responsibilities assimilated from the literature (Appendix E.1-E.4). The insurance CIO spent 91% of his verbal contact time in four of these areas of responsibility:

Responsibility area	% of time	% of occurrences
Strategic planning	43	7
Coordination of 3 groups	19	28
Other general managerial	21	33
Approval, acceptance of expenditure	8	19

Of the five CIOs observed, the insurance CIO devoted the highest percentage of his time to the other day-to-day general managerial activities. The university CIO was next highest, and the others were significantly lower. The university CIO's second-in-command position was open and had been for six months.

Strategic planning activities constitute only 7% of the insurance company CIO's verbal contacts but account for 43% of verbal contact time. Three scheduled meetings, two with senior management and one with senior management and a vendor, dominated this time. Desk work associated with these meetings was also coded with this responsibility. The first meeting, which lasted five hours, was called by the CEO. Attended by the CEO, First Senior VP, and four other Senior VPs including the CIO, this session was intended to be an open-ended think session. Considerations were environmental forces and degree of control over these forces as well as strengths and weaknesses within the organization. Basic questions were asked: Where are we? Where are we going for the 1990s? The CEO discussed three facets of operating success in the 1990s: quality, flexibility, and speed. Twenty steps to assure success were listed. The group determined that service was a major success factor which the company could control and decided that the company should provide a level of service "measurably but not extraordinarily better than the competition." The principles of risk management were reviewed.

A follow-up meeting was held the next morning during which specific strategies to add value were discussed and assignments made. The CIO prepared a folder for reference before the first meeting and studied the minutes of the first meeting before attending the second meeting. These desk work sessions took place during his early morning quiet time.

One full day was devoted to visiting the vendor of an image processing system. The CIO traveled on the company plane with the Senior VP of Administration and two Vice Presidents, who reported to the Senior VP of Administration. The Second Vice President of the ISD and the ISD project leader met this group at the vendor's headquarters. This system was under review in the context of strategic planning. Not only would it cut labor costs in policy assembly but it would also decrease the time to put a policy in the hands of a new customer. According to marketing, this turnaround would lower the number of customers who change their minds and decide not to enroll. The flexibility of the relational databases also provided the opportunity to provide new products easily and even to make computing services one of these products. The quality of customer service would also be improved, allowing customer service personnel to retrieve policies quickly on the screen which look like the paper copy used by the customer. This system would also lower the errors associated with policy issuance and maintenance. Thus, the project embodied the three facets for success in the 1990s identified by the CEO: speed, flexibility, and quality.

Coordinating activities among the three groups—the environment or external, the ISD or information technology unit, and functional areas—ranked third among the responsibilities in terms of time consumed and second in terms of the number of occurrences. Examples of coordinating activities are conducting an unscheduled meeting with the manager of the Japan branch's ISD, reviewing the image processing system product during a meeting with members of the ISD staff, talking with the facilities manager regarding problems in the Data Center, talking with the operations manager regarding a vendor's back-up equipment used during the data center move, discussing the image processing trip with a Senior VP, and talking with human resources about golf league participation for the ISD.

Approval or acceptance of expenditures constituted nineteen percent of all verbal contacts but only 8% of contact time. However, mail was dominated by approval or acceptance of expenses (32%) followed by coordination of the three groups (22%).

Roles Analysis

Following Mintzberg's role definitions, the CIO acted as liaison when interacting with those outside the IT unit and as leader when interacting only with those inside the unit. Liaison and leader seemed to be of almost equal importance.

Verbal Contacts

The insurance company CIO acted as a liaison or interface with other functional units and the environment during 56% of his verbal contact time. On an occurrence basis, the liaison role accounted for 36% of all verbal contacts and 42% of all nonverbal occurrences or pieces of mail. The leader role then accounted for 44% of contact time, 64% of contact occurrences, and 58% of all mail.

Decisional roles were more important than informational roles. The insurance company CIO spent 25% of verbal time playing informational roles and 69% playing decisional roles. The strategic decisional roles—entrepreneur and resource allocator—accounted for 60% of the CIO's time versus 48% on average for the five CIOs. The entrepreneur role is linked with strategic planning—particularly the day spent evaluating the image processing system and the open-ended strategic planning sessions in which the objective was to add value using existing resources and computing capacity.

The remaining two decisional roles, disturbance handler and negotiator, consumed only 8% of the CIO's time compared to 21% on average. These roles may have been affected by the presence of a Second Vice President, who seemed to handle many of the day-to-day problems, and by the CIO's high percentage of self-initiated contacts. He made an effort to be open and available to ISD members on their territory frequently. Conflicts may have been nipped in the bud by this accessibility. Furthermore, his demeanor was that of a peacemaker: unemotional, unbiased, open to suggestions, but firm with decisions made. With senior executives and functional managers who might have felt threatened by the rather sudden strategic importance which information systems had acquired, the CIO played the role of a humble, personable "techie," glad to guide them through the difficulties of using information technology, not forgetting that he was a newcomer to the group.

He also represented the view of the opposing party in enemy territory, so to speak, keeping exchange open.   At the ISD meeting attended by all ISD employees, he told them that the CEO had challenged the company to work toward goals that were possible only through the application of information technology.   He emphasized that top management realized that the ISD must play a pivotal role:

> In some insurance companies, the 4 A's—actuarial, accounting, administrative, agency—plan and then ask, Who will tell the computer guy?   In these companies, the computer guys inhibit the use of computers, not enhance it.   To play a pivotal role, the computer group must be sensitive to its customers.

He reviewed the customer service survey and discussed the problem of project date deadlines not being met in terms of demand outweighing supply.   He countered this fact with an example from the customer's viewpoint.   When he had experienced an electronic mail problem this morning, that problem had become his most important priority. Knowing that the person who could help was busy did not satisfy him.   He reminded the employees that they were actively seeking programmers, consultants, and independent contractors.   He emphasized, however, the real answer was a long-term objective:

> returning the demand to the requester through departmental computers for the 4 A's running systems so constructed that system users can perform queries and maintain the systems by editing parameters for procedural changes. But how successful are we going to be going to the customer and saying we have a long-term solution?   Not very successful.   I suspect that I've lost touch.   I suspect that this is a perception our customers have of all of us.

The ISD meeting described was coded disseminator role since this was its primary purpose.   However, its preventive value in terms of conflict resolution is obvious.   The CIO seemed especially adept at perceiving situations from others' viewpoints and communicating on that basis.

Roles were analyzed by medium to determine if certain mediums and roles seemed to be associated or if CIOs chose certain mediums to play certain roles. For the insurance CIO, two thirds of meeting time was devoted to the entrepreneurial role.   The four decisional roles constituted almost 80% of his scheduled meeting time (Appendix H.2).

Unscheduled meeting time was 54% decisional and 45% informational (Appendix H.3).   The CIO used unscheduled meetings as a means of staying in touch, with the informational roles in this medium representing the highest percentage among the verbal mediums and being close to that of desk work, 48%.

Telephone calls were 77% decisional, with resource allocation being a dominant role. Fifty-four percent of telephone time was consumed by acceptance/rejection of proposed use of time or materials. Examples of the CIO's resource allocation phone calls include scheduling a trip to Japan, scheduling his time and that of four subordinates, allocating his own time by confirming that he will attend a meeting but only for 30 minutes, and making a decision on the leave status (affecting salary) of an employee.

Desk Work

Three roles—resource allocator, monitor, and disseminator—accounted for 82% of mail occurrences. Sixty-one percent of the incoming mail involved resource allocation. Output mail (Appendix H.7) was just the opposite. Only 32% percent involved decisional roles. Sixty-four percent involved informational roles with 50% being "Disseminator."

Verbal Contacts and Desk Work

Scheduled meetings were identified with the entrepreneur role. The resource allocator role was the most frequent role for unscheduled meetings, telephone calls, and incoming mail. Incoming mail tended to require decisional roles and outgoing, informational roles. The disseminator role was the most frequent for outgoing mail. Most disturbance handling was conducted during unscheduled meetings, as would be expected since disturbance handling involves crises which cannot wait. However, the CIO used unscheduled meetings primarily for informational roles.

8

The Government Installation CIO

BACKGROUND

The Installation

The core business of the government installation is to manage science and engineering projects related to space transportation and exploration. This installation is one of 14 field centers of an agency with headquarters located in Washington, D.C. The relationship of field centers to each other resembles a matrix structure. Responsibility and authority are shifted by projects and areas of expertise. For example, this particular center's major responsibility is for propulsion systems but it also has a lead responsibility for telecommunications—the voice, data, and image network employed by all field centers and headquarters. The relationship of sites to headquarters in Washington is decentralized, and field centers have a great deal of autonomy.

The Director of the field center has three direct reports as well as project offices and staff services such as the center comptroller, chief counsel, and equal opportunity office. These three direct reports head (1) the program development effort, which is essentially a marketing arm; (2) a science and engineering function which provides in-house technical support to projects; and (3) an institutional and program support function. The CIO or Director of the Information Systems Office (ISO) reports to the Director of Institutional and Program Support, who reports to the Site Director. The CIO's experience was primarily in communications, for which this field center had the lead responsibility for the agency.

The Information Systems Office (ISO)

Three chiefs report to the CIO or Director of ISO: (1) systems development and implementation, (2) network management, and (3) systems and network engineering or technical services. The CIO also has operational responsibility for a remote computer complex. The systems development chief has responsibility for three groups: Engineering Systems, Data Systems, and Operations and Maintenance. The data systems are essentially administrative systems. This field center has lead responsibility for an agency-wide accounting system which cost tens of millions of dollars to develop. The network management chief has a matrix responsibility position. Those who support network management in operations and engineering work through him. He also has direct responsibility for telecommunications requirements review and planning for all agency field centers. A resource management unit, reporting to the network chief, determines what agency and contractor resources will be required and budgeted for the agency-wide network.

The network managed at this center is global in scope. Nineteen agency sites, nearly 60 colleges and universities, over 200 contractor locations, and sites in Europe, the former Soviet Union, Japan, and Canada are included. Voice, data, and video are transmitted and videoconferencing provides a valuable tool for day-to-day business and the coordination of recovery missions.

The ISO has an annual budget of over $150 million and is located in two buildings at the center. With about 75 employees, the ISO manages the activities of more than 1200 contractor employees. This relationship with contractors is a critical part of the CIO's job. Because of rigid government job classifications, selections, and promotion regulations, legal issues involving civil service employees are also critical. For example, the CIO related that his secretary was capable of doing more administrative work but her job classification would have to be changed which would require extensive approval since the ISO already had an administrative assistant.

In addition to the layering of civil service and contractor employees and the unclear lines of responsibility in many matrix situations, the CIO also had to deal with the lag between action and reaction in the technology acquisition area. He commented that technology moved faster than the authorities for expenditure, which often made the approved purchase obsolete. As part of the agency's commitment to Total Quality, the CIO had begun to implement procedure changes whereby documents were processed concurrently instead of sequentially. He also had begun a study of documents that he is required to sign to determine whether that step is necessary or whether authority could be granted closer to the request.

For this CIO, a typical week consisted of many routine or scheduled meetings and activities. The CIO commented that the content of the week observed was atypical in two respects. First, more attention was paid to the executive personnel selection process because of the announcement of the CIO's new Deputy Director. Second, a regularly scheduled Wednesday morning network meeting was canceled to attend a Total Quality meeting. Using a calendar for four weeks, scheduled meetings comprised 58% of a 40-hour work; during the observation week, scheduled meetings constituted 56% of observed time.

The CIO was very conscious of time management and the structure of the work week. More than other CIOs, he was aware of what the observer would need to know and talked through mail and other one way communications such as phone calls. During travel time with the observer, he explained events which would be difficult to understand without further information.

The CIO held a B.S., M.S., and Ph.D. in industrial engineering, had been an associate professor in Engineering Management, and had worked as a project engineer and as a systems analyst. At the field center, he had been an executive staff officer and assistant to the Director. He had moved through the ranks of the ISO and served as Deputy Director of Computer Services and Director of Communications. Between these two positions, he served as Chairman of the Source Evaluation Board, which plays a critical role in selecting contractors for approved projects. After the restructuring which combined computer and communications functions, he served as Deputy Director of the ISO and then became the Director. He had been at the field center for twenty years. He had received an Outstanding Performance Award and a prestigious NASA Leadership Medal.

The CIO had extensive contacts throughout the field center and agency as well as in-depth knowledge of how contractors work. He had been involved in the field center's Center Council, which formulated the center's strategic plan. His advanced degrees were not uncommon among this group. Many of the science and engineering managers and project managers had doctorates, according to the CIO.

The CIO knew his calendar before the day began and was successful in controlling his time. He wanted a meeting agenda prior to all scheduled meetings. His office was arranged so that his desk formed one end of a conference table, which allowed convenient access to files and phone. His secretary was located within sight and hearing distance of his desk in an adjacent office. Entrance to his office was through his secretary's office.

The CIO completed desk work in a sitting rather than in snatches. is secretary sorted his mail into three folders: for signature only, for information only, and hold, which was a reading file. He completed the "for signature only" file while he ate lunch at his desk. He returned phone calls immediately, and his messages did not accumulate. His secretary often had others handle phone calls directed to him. Before tackling a problem referred to him, he asked for a thorough review of what had been done to "work the problem." He told me he wanted to force responsibility down in the ranks, not force every decision to be made at the top. He tried to avoid taking work home and preferred to separate the two spheres.

While the CIO made a conscious effort to manage his time and avoid distractions, he did not do so by shutting out detail that might be important.

After a videoconference with headquarters, he immediately went to the control room and requested the videotape of the conference. A small, lighted sign on a panel had indicated that the videoconference was being taped. The operator from whom he requested the tape had replied, "I told them you'd ask for it." Following the conference, the CIO phoned the headquarter's network coordinator, who had participated in the videoconference. He conveyed his belief that the contractor who provided the contract service of videoconferencing had told the operator to tape the conference so they could review it. This was not appropriate since the contractor was currently under review by the General Services Administration. According to the CIO, "the innocent comment, 'I told them you'd ask for that,' told me a lot." The CIO held staff meetings on an ISO policy manual and Information Resource Oversight Council statement of purpose, policy, responsibilities, goals, objective, and strategies. The emphasis in both meetings was on the detailed, precise use of words to shape policy or purpose. The CIO told the ISO staff that the policy manual would take "detailed attention . . . it may seem like a bottomless pit." This attention to detail also applied to routine desk work. He returned a newsletter for correction because the newsletter indicated that ISO employees had accompanied contractor employees to a seminar. Because he promoted the concept that contractor employees were part of ISO as well as civil service employees, his note read, "?—contractor employees ARE ISO employees."

An examination of operating procedures and information resource management was critical for the CIO. Systems integration had become a significant problem for the agency because project groups used specialized workstations and software but required access to the network. Although information systems development and implementation support was primarily in the administrative area, the project area was supported through the communications unit. To access the network, some standards had to be adopted and security measures enforced. For the autonomous and highly skilled research groups in the project area, standards were often an obstacle. In a shared research environment, security measures were often a nuisance.

The agency as a whole was struggling to harness the information resources at its disposal. Further complicating this effort was the inevitable difference in the administrative and project points of view. The situation at this agency resembled the administrative and academic computing scenario at the university.

THE OBSERVATION WEEK

Four topics dominated the observation week: (1) executive personnel selection process, (2) review of a major contract, (3) information resource management policy, and (4) Total Quality approach applied to processes within the ISO. In addition to the usual considerations, the selection process at the field center required the chief counsel's input and approval. The chief counsel of the center was heavily involved in executive personnel selection and studied each candidate and had to agree on the candidate selected. Since the computer services unit and communications unit were combined, one consideration for the Deputy Director position was that this person be associated with computer services since the Director or CIO was from communications most recently. During the observation week, the Director of the Information Systems Office reviewed the selection he had made with the Director of Institutional and Program Support. He then met personally with each applicant not selected to explain the selection rationale. Several phone conversations touched on the selection of a deputy as well. Desk work involved an announcement on the selection. The CIO used the selection process to demonstrate the value he placed on confidentiality. Not even his secretary knew who had been selected as deputy. After he talked with each applicant, he seemed to listen for leaks as if testing for them.

The second major topic of the observation week at the government installation was the Government Service Administration review of a major contract for rebid. Although communications and computer services had been combined, two contracts existed for these services even though the same company held both contracts. Savings could be realized by combining contracts. Recompeting the contract involved major costs. The present contractor had spent $5 million to prepare its proposal and the center had spent 30 personnel-years reviewing the bids.

The CIO's doctoral research had involved predicting cost trends on contracts for launch vehicles. As Chairman of the Source Evaluation Board for the current communication contract, he had responsibility for developing and evaluating proposals and then selecting contractors to implement proposals. The ISO wanted to combine the contracts but also wanted to alter some conditions to give the contractor a greater sense of mission responsibility and increased incentive to perform. The relationship with contractors was one of oversight and monitoring as well as partnership. Having the contract with the agency provided the contractor a prestige and marketing edge in private industry, both in the United States and abroad. The CIO used this fact, along with the contract itself, to control and provide incentives for the performance of the contractor.

In dealing with the General Services Administration and contractors, the CIO needed to be able to discern what the driving issues were and who was driving these issues. Many phone conversations involved how a certain person reacted or who knew what when. As the CIO told the headquarters network coordinator, a little often told him a lot when dealing with contractors. He cultivated the relationship of partner but did not ignore the possibility of conflicting interests or his responsibility to manage contractor performance since the contractor played a major role in accomplishing the ISO mission.

The third major issue during the week was information resource management (IRM). Six meetings involved this issue. On Monday, the Government

Accounting Office (GAO) requested an IRM audit entrance meeting. Auditors
from the Information Management and Technology Division of the GAO were
performing a three-month IRM survey of the agency, visiting headquarters and
two major centers. During this meeting, the auditors explained that their
approach would be to interview and obtain documentation. IRM would be a
major effort at the GAO. The GAO believed that a data dictionary must be an
agency-wide effort to realize economies of storage, an increasingly important
issue. The center's chief counsel attended the meeting because regulatory
violations could be involved in how the agency handles information. A Science
and Engineering information resource manager, the Deputy Comptroller, the
Deputy Director of Institutional and Program Support, and the head of internal
auditing for the agency attended the meeting. The Director of ISO, the CIO,
commented that he thought responsibility for software standards needed to be
clarified. At this field center, the Quality Assurance office had responsibility
for standards, yet this office was concerned primarily with flight safety and
reliability not software for administrative and program support or for the
network which everyone accessed. Each project and technology/engineering
group had its own specialized programmers. Even with this diversity, a
common architecture needed to be in place whenever feasible. Security of
information resources also needed to be addressed in the research and development environment.

The second meeting was attended by a technical writer, the CIO, and the chief
of Systems Engineering. A draft of an IRM policy document was discussed and
revised. A third meeting to review the document containing these revisions was
scheduled and held. During a fourth IRM meeting, IRM auditors from the GAO
interviewed the CIO and his new Deputy. The fifth meeting was an audit exit
meeting with the GAO auditors. A sixth meeting was scheduled by the Director
of Institutional and Program Support.

At this sixth meeting, a consulting group presented its proposal for performing
an IRM assessment at the center. The division Director asked the CIO for his
comments after the presentation. He replied that he believed the ISO needed to
use its resources to implement the ideas already in place instead of doing more
studies. He asserted that the interview strategy proposed to identify needs was
invalid: "This is the old problem of how to get requirements. We know that
you can't just sit down with people and get requirements." He concluded that
the ISO was already doing what the consultants proposed. The real need was
systems integration for what already existed. The Director listened, nodded, and
scheduled no follow-up with the consultants.

This meeting was held at the center's headquarters building. Traveling back
to the ISO building, the CIO commented that he hoped they could see how upset
he had been about this proposal. I was surprised to learn the CIO had been
upset. He had not changed expression, voice tone, volume, or gestures. His
response had seemed unbiased and calm. He had not become distracted by any

side issue. Indeed, he seemed a good fit for an installation whose core business was science and engineering projects.

The fourth major issue during the observation week was the Total Quality approach applied to the ISO. The CIO and his chiefs attended a seminar on the Total Quality approach conducted by a prominent national consultant. The CIO followed up on the seminar, devoting a portion of the staff meeting to improving standard operating procedures and issuances.

Chronology Record

This CIO was observed for only 35.5 hours because of vacation time taken Friday afternoon (attention required for a family matter which the CIO was not aware of when the observation week was scheduled). Fifty-six percent of the CIO's time was spent in scheduled meetings lasting an average of 44 minutes each (compared to a 59-minute average for all CIOs). Fourteen percent of his time was spent in unscheduled meetings. Despite the volume of the CIO's mail, he spent only 15% (Appendix A.1) of his time on desk work. He spent the same percentage of time on telephone calls, and he experienced the highest number of telephone calls. Thus, 70% of the CIO's time was spent in meetings and 30% on desk work and calls.

Verbal Contacts

Although 44% of verbal contacts (Appendix A.2) were phone calls, only 17% of contact time was devoted to phone calls. On the other hand, 23% of contacts were scheduled meetings, but 65% of contact time was devoted to scheduled meetings. Scheduled and unscheduled meetings made meeting time 82% of verbal contact time. Fifty-nine percent of total participants were subordinates; 6% superiors and 17% internal peers. Eighteen percent were vendors. The CIO initiated almost half of all contacts. Seventy-nine percent of all contacts occurred in his office. He preferred to remain in place, with smooth transitions between activities. The fact that his office was arranged as a conference room facilitated the use of his office for most meetings. Over half of his government scheduled meetings had four or more people. However, 84% of unscheduled meetings involved only one other person.

Incoming Mail

The memo was the dominant form of incoming mail (61%) (Appendix A.3). Letters were 9% compared to an average of 17%. Memos were further categorized into announcements, authorization forms, and e-mail (Appendix D.3). An analysis of these subcategories shows the government agency CIO receiving a higher percentage of authorization forms and announcements. The government CIO skimmed 83% of his mail.

The sender of incoming mail (Appendix B.3) was usually a subordinate (76%) although mail did come from a superior (3%), internal peers (7%), and vendors (7%). Using Mintzberg's categories of mail purpose, the mail was fairly evenly split between request and informational. This CIO did not make extensive use of electronic mail (5%), largely because of the high number of authorization forms which required a legal signature.

Outgoing Mail

During the observation week, the government agency CIO was not a writer. A major policy document was written by a technical writer and staff chief. The CIO used scheduled meetings to convey his intentions and work on specific revisions. His output as a percent of input was eight percent (Appendix B.4). He responded to input for 70% of outgoing mail. Eighty percent of outgoing mail went to subordinates. Memos were forty percent of outgoing mail and thirty percent was simply a forwarding of input mail. One writing session consisted of a report for strategic planning written at home and another, a letter to the Director, was edited. Ninety-nine percent of desk work occurrences were in the government agency CIO's office (Appendix D.2).

Activity Durations

Eighty-three percent of activities lasted 30 minutes or less and over half (53%) lasted five minutes or less (Appendix C). The brevity of over half the activities observed at the government agency did not indicate a frenzied, hectic, unpredictable, or driven pace, however. On the contrary, one of the reasons for brevity was the CIO's control of meeting time, insistence on agendas for meetings, and organization of desk work into action folders.

Interaction Analysis

Fifty-five percent of verbal contacts and 43% of desk work occurrences were with areas outside the information technology unit (Appendix H.7 and Appendix D.1).

Responsibility Analysis

Three responsibilities accounted for 72% percent of the CIO's contact time (Appendix E.1):

1. Coordination of the three groups

2. Approval/acceptance of expenditure
3. Policies, procedures, and guidelines

Strategic planning accounted for only 7% of contact time. Information resource management work was categorized as "Policy, procedures, and guidelines." The CIO had the highest percentage of time in this category but the lowest percentage for strategic planning.

On an occurrence basis, the ranking for the top three responsibility areas of desk work (Appendix E.2) was expenditures, coordination, and other managerial. Environmental scanning was the lowest among the five CIOs, probably because the Director of Institutional and Program Support had assigned new technology to his staff deputy.

For all occurrences (Appendix E.3), almost 80% of verbal contacts and pieces of mail were in the same three areas of responsibility: expenditures (39%), coordination (24%), and other managerial (16%).

Roles Analysis

Verbal Contacts

Analysis of verbal contact roles (Appendix F.1) showed that the CIO played informational roles for almost a third of his contact time and decisional roles for about two thirds. The role of resource allocator accounted for almost half of all contact occurrences. Disturbance handler was the next most dominant role, followed by disseminator. The CIO played the disturbance handler role was played primarily during telephone calls and unscheduled meetings.

Desk Work

Eighty-three percent of desk work occurrences (Appendix F.5) involved three roles: resource allocation, monitor, and spokesman. The CIO played informational roles for 43% of occurrences. Outgoing mail, however, was 70% informational with 30% assigned to monitor; 20%, disseminator; and 20% spokesman. Resource allocation was still a major category at 30% of occurrences.

Verbal Contacts and Desk Work

For all mail and contacts on an occurrence basis, information roles were about one third and decisional roles two thirds. The resource allocator role accounted for almost half of all occurrences.

9

The Utility Company CIO

BACKGROUND

Company

With $20 billion in total assets and annual revenues exceeding $7 billion, the electric utility company discussed in this chapter is a major player in the utility industry. The utility company is publicly regulated so that geographical areas and rates are restricted. Furthermore, public regulation requires the utility company to be extremely sensitive to public relations and to sustain a lobbying effort at the state and national level. The utility company stock is traded on the New York Stock Exchange (NYSE) as a stable stock from which investors can expect a reasonable dividend. The median age of stockholders is 66. Over half have held the shares for more than 10 years, and almost 60% have acquired additional shares since initial purchase.

The holding company is organized by regulatory requirements into five electric utility operating companies, a nuclear power operating company, and a services company, which provides charge-back services on a competitive basis for the operating companies. Each operating company must adhere to a state regulatory commission and remain within a designated territory, usually a state. Operating companies, with the exception of the nuclear power company, produced the same product in much the same way. Two operating companies are dominant, one generating half of total revenues and the other generating a third. Regulations prohibit much direct control of operating companies by the holding company, to which the services unit is attached directly. The service company's President and CEO report directly to the holding company's President, who, in turns, reports to the Board of Directors. The President and CEOs of operating companies report to their own Board of Directors and the holding company President. Operating company CEOs act with a high degree of autonomy.

According to the holding company President, the conception of a utility company as a player in a monopoly market with guaranteed profits is outdated: "Competition will come from independent power producers (IPPs) selling to large industrial users." Independent power producers have been encouraged by the federal government, according to the annual report. They "build and operate power plants for one or more customers." In one state, customers over a specified size can choose their energy supplier. According to the President, this experience has been an indicator of what the future may be like in other states. The company captured 73% of these customer-choice jobs.

However, just as deregulation of the communications environment caused significant change within participating organizations, the President foresees the need for a quick change within the utility company: "We began changing our company's culture—because our industry is changing." A new vision statement was written and restructuring begun. The Information Resource Organization (IRO) within the services company was a key player in this restructuring. In fact, restructuring to effect a culture change was the major concern of the observation week. According to the vision statement presented to all 30,000 employees:

The . . . electric system has developed a heritage of reliable supply and responsive service. We are the major source of electric energy in the Southeast.

But now we face growing competitive pressures. Our markets are being opened to a host of competing suppliers, and a significant share of our revenues will be at risk in the 1990s. To ensure our future—to solidify our position as a quality, low-cost producer—and to seize the opportunities of this new era—we must change. We must operate our system to gain the full benefit of our strengths.

The vision statement announced top management's commitment to "establish clearer lines of authority and accountability for results," to "build a culture that rewards independent thinking and quicker decision making." Accordingly, "open and honest communication will form the basis of all our business relationships."

In the former culture, layoffs or dismissals for poor performance were taboo. Now the company had implemented "right sizing." Jobs for over 80 managers were eliminated. Layers of management between the top and the plant floor were reduced from seven to four. Performance evaluations became more important. According to the CIO, "the utility culture had been that you never fired anyone." During the past two years, the IRO had terminated 58 people for poor performance: "Tough guidelines were implemented." A five-level review was used. If an employee received a fourth-level or below review for two consecutive years, the employee was terminated for poor performance. In the meanwhile, one operating company consolidated eight data centers into two with a net present value savings of $8 million, according to the CIO.

The present structure blocked many of the advantages of producing the same product. Each operating company had its own information systems, each performing very similar functions. Tension existed between the operating companies which wanted to maintain autonomy, and the holding company, which wanted to take advantage of similarities to provide common functions at a reduced cost. The IRO was being used as a "bellwether" for restructuring, according to the CIO.

The Information Resource Organization

Each operating company had its own IRO, but the IRO attached to the service company was the largest unit, with 720 employees after "right sizing." Within the year, the CIO, as Senior Vice President of Information Resources, had begun to report to the President of the services company instead of to the Executive Vice President of Finance. Subsequently, he was named Chief Information Officer for the holding company as well as Senior Vice President for the services company. He was a member of the Management Council, the group of senior executives for all operating companies, the service company, and the holding company. In this position he would have responsibility for all IROs and could oversee a coherent architecture and shared systems. This assimilation was the company's first attempt at restructuring reporting relationships as a means to change its culture and improve its competitiveness. IRO's had previously reported to an operating company executive and the service company IRO could only "jawbone" to exert influence, according to the CIO.

During the observation week, the top priorities on the CIO's agenda were to establish the provisions for this new structure and to unify the IROs. The CIO, who had been with the utility company for 27 years, told me that he believed he had one year to "make a difference. If no difference, no job." Noticing my shock, he continued, "Having a job at risk is not a bad place to be because it makes you work harder and smarter."

The CIO seemed to have fulfilled the poet Robert Burns's wish to see himself as others saw him and to understand the position of others as if he were in their place. This empathy seemed to be the source of much goodwill and loyalty as well as a key to his ability to sell his program. One operating company IRO manager told him that it was the goodwill he had throughout the organization that could make the restructuring work.

For a subordinate who was voicing his frustration at continuing opposition from a powerful executive, the CIO delineated the executive's position so convincingly that the subordinate became unsure of his own position. Then the CIO pointed out an approach which would accommodate both points of view and alleviate the executive's fear of damage to his organization. After a week of meetings full of turf protection, resistance, and some bickering, I asked the CIO how he had avoided ever getting angry. He replied that his years of negotiating with regulators in Washington and then negotiating with labor had taught him that the person who gets angry loses.

The CIO had earned his undergraduate degree at the U.S. Military Academy at West Point. He commented that the discipline and knowledge of military strategy acquired there had been helpful. He began his career with the utility company after military school as a junior engineer. He was sent to Washington to provide technical expertise on regulations and then to negotiate himself. His success in negotiating with regulators led the company to place him in employee relations where he negotiated with labor unions. From there, he was promoted in the Human Resources area. The CIO told me that he had received an unsolicited but tempting offer from another company. The utility company responded by making him responsible for administration, including the MIS area. He commented that the decision to give him the MIS area had probably been on the basis of his being the user who "bitched the loudest." Nevertheless, he became heavily involved in this area. He finds that human resource issues are still the dominant concerns of his job.

The restructuring now under way had been on the CIO's agenda from the beginning, but for six years the "political climate" of the organization would have meant failure: "I had to bide my time until the climate was right for acceptance." During this time, the CIO earned an M.B.A. from an Executive M.B.A. program in the same city and attended the prestigious Stanford Executive program for two months at Stanford. He told me that he returned to school when he felt he had reached a plateau and must keep growing. The "having arrived" feeling some executives acquire when they move into the executive wing can cause them to quit functioning, he added.

The CIO's office was in the executive floor of the holding company, where the President of the holding company, President and CEO of the services company, and executive conference room were also located. Wood panelling, dark hardwood floors, oriental rugs, and traditional antique furniture had created an atmosphere of stability and prestige. The CIO commented that the surroundings on the executive floor might intimidate some members of the IRO, but at this time, his location on this floor was important. However, he was considering moving to the building where the IRO was housed at a later time. He felt a degree of isolation in his present location.

His office had a formal and informal area. Across from his desk were guest chairs. Side chairs were against the wall behind these guest chairs and in front of the informal seating area (a sofa, two chairs, and coffee table). These side chairs could be pulled forward to the desk for additional seating or to the informal area to accommodate six people there.

The CIO arrived at work at least one hour before the normal workday began. He checked his electronic mail, voice mail, operational reports from an

Executive Support System, and a report showing the company's stock price along with that of 15 other utility companies, the Dow Jones Industrial Index, the S&P 500 Index, the Dow Jones Utility Index, and the NYSE Utility Index. He used an AT&T touch screen telephone for voice mail and for dialing. Frequently used numbers were on one screen. Other numbers were available through menus or alphabetically in pages, with screens resembling the phone book. He also used a cellular phone for returning and receiving calls on his way to and from work and during travel.

Electronic mail was an important communication tool for this CIO. He told me that people will use electronic mail to ask questions they won't ask over the phone. Each month, he sends an electronic mail letter to the over 700 IRO employees. He asks for questions and comments via electronic mail and is pleased with the response he gets: "Every time I send a letter out, I get 25 to 30 e-mail notes back—thank you, questions, suggestions. It's one way I can build camaraderie in an organization this big. I used to know everyone's name."

He had encouraged the use of the Executive Support System among the inner circle of executives on the executive floor. So far, he had won over three executives and was working on the President. Certainly, he set the example in its use. The electronic mail and Executive Support System was now on a MacIntosh terminal. When the terminal was not in use, a screen saver graphics program ran in the background, forming visually pleasing designs and drawing attention to the terminal. The CIO also had a closed circuit TV on which he could access weather maps, company news, and national news, or view videotapes. The weather map, which was updated periodically remained on the television screen. Surrounding the CIO's traditional executive desk were three screens, all lit and all used comfortably. Like the university CIO who had begun his involvement with information technology as a user, this CIO remained a highly visible user of information technology.

The CIO seemed to pay particular attention to the timing of events, treating timing as a critical factor and being aware of the cost in time of a delayed decision. He was adamant that a decision on the provisions of restructuring be made by a certain date. He told his assistant, "It's critical to get on [Management Council Agenda] Monday. We're doomed to fail if we sit in a holding pattern [for 4 weeks]. Walls will be built." Later, he commented, "We need to get on [the agenda] by 3:30 P.M. By 4:00 P.M., they may not want to make a decision—they'll be thinking about home." He was put on the agenda, but at 4:30 P.M. One operating company CEO would not make a decision, as the CIO had anticipated would happen with this timing. Thus, the CIO volunteered to meet with this one CEO later but pressed to make the timing within the next two work days. When the CEO stalled, saying his calendar was full for the next two days, the CIO agreed that this might be a problem and suggested meeting Friday after 5 P.M. when both calendars would probably be clear. The CIO was adamant that a delay at this juncture was critical.

THE OBSERVATION WEEK

The CIO's first activity was to check his terminals for voice and electronic mail and the reports on the Executive Support System. Then he reviewed his list of things to do. Each afternoon, he made a fresh list before leaving for home. He accomplished most desk work in between times for other events rather than at a prespecified time, although he did arrive an hour early for quiet time. This first hour usually allowed for uninterrupted desk work. His administrative assistant filtered all his desk work, eliminating an estimated three quarters of it. She placed the remaining mail into three colored folders. The red folder was a signature folder; yellow, priority mail; and green, general information. He processed the mail in red, yellow, and green order and kept a reference folder. He took this reference folder with him to read while traveling.

The CIO worked methodically and steadily. He underlined and highlighted mail as he read it. He separated mail for the trash can and mail for recyclable waste. His administrative assistant also filtered his phone calls. Her phone as well as his terminal indicated the number and name of all internal callers before the phone rang. She also filtered unscheduled meetings and meeting requests, often probing for details of the meeting to determine whether the CIO should attend. Unless participants in meetings were frequent contacts, she announced the name and area for each participant before escorting them to the formal or informal area.

The CIO and his administrative assistant worked as partners, discussing events and the implications of events. They had worked together for almost 10 years. She kept his calendar up-to-date on the electronic mail system and printed a desk copy for his use at least once a day. His calendar was accessible by other users of the electronic mail system. This CIO was the only one whose calendar was available through the electronic mail system.

The services company IRO had six managers reporting directly to the CIO during the observation week: Director of Information Systems, Director of Computer Services, Director of Information Network Services, Manager of Information Resources Plans and Controls, Manager of Data Administration, and Information Resource Technology Coordinator. With the restructuring, the information resource managers for six operating companies would report to him as well. These managers at the two largest operating companies were vice presidents. At the smaller operating companies, these managers reported to administrative vice presidents, who had other responsibilities as well. In addition, pockets of functional areas information resource personnel existed in engineering and other areas.

A question raised with restructuring was the CIO's span of control. He would have 12 direct reports, six of them at geographically dispersed locations and four of them out of state. Moreover, at the smaller companies, the information resource manager needed to report to someone who would make decisions on a day-to-day basis. The responsibilities of these direct reports were more operational. Since layers of management had just been reduced, no one wanted this restructuring to add a layer of management.

The Management Council had asked the CIO to present restructuring proposals along with advantages and disadvantages of each. He had talked with Management Council members and several information resource managers. He had three alternatives and had decided on the one he preferred. He needed the Management Council's agreement on this alternative during the observation week so that he could begin to make changes immediately before resistance to change strengthened.

This restructuring and its implementation gave coherence to the week's main activities. Considering whether this week was fairly typical, the CIO said that the meetings and activities were of utmost importance during the week but that his work habits had remained the same. His administrative assistant agreed. The CIO spent 49% of his time in scheduled meetings during the observation week. Using his calendar for four weeks, an estimated 45% of his time was spent in scheduled meetings.

On the first observation day, the CIO met with a subordinate on the restructuring presentation for the Management Council meeting, thanked company managers who organized a community benefit by hosting a luncheon for them at his private club, and met with auditors to clarify the implications of the restructuring for them. As a board member of a telecommunications company, he studied an acquisition proposal. The utility company had joint ventures with this telecommunications company; it provided them with right of ways for fiber optic lines for a fee and used these lines for its own network. The CIO caught up on mail and made a decision on job levels to which company cellular phones could be assigned.

On the second day, he flew to a neighboring state to meet the VP of the IRO and assistant to the President/CEO of one of the big two operating companies. He discussed restructuring, listened to their concerns, and gained their support prior to the Management Council meeting. Before returning to his office to attend two more scheduled meetings, he toured the Data Center with the VP and was introduced by the VP as the CIO of the operating company as well as the entire company. That afternoon, he again met with an assistant to discuss the restructuring presentation and wording for the forthcoming announcement. He met with the internal systems auditors again and listened to their concerns. He suggested that they hire technical people and teach them auditing skills. Auditing systems increasingly required some technical skills, especially with regard to security. At the company airport, the CIO used a PC terminal tied into the company's network to check his electronic mail.

The CIO spent the third day with a utility company operating outside the geographical boundaries of his company. He investigated a new product opportunity which would enable the company to use present utility systems for value-added services. He told me that he had scheduled this all-day, out-of-state meeting on this day so that he would be difficult to contact on the day before the critical management meeting. He believed that support could be gained in some companies by sharing information, as he had done the day before. In other operating companies, information was just ammunition for the resistance effort. The scheduling of this all-day meeting was a graceful way of avoiding unwanted questions. He used plane travel time to read the contents of his green folder, and in this case, to chat with systems analysts who accompanied him on this trip.

The CIO worked on avoiding isolation. During the past year following "right sizing," he had met with every member of the services company IRO for lunch in groups of 15 to 20. He said that people would ask questions in these small groups but not in groups of 100. His administrative assistant had attended each of the approximately 40 lunch meetings and completed a list of suggestions for improvement, many of which were currently being implemented. This trip was the first one that many of the systems analysts had taken on the company plane. The CIO worked to put them at ease and make them comfortable. He listened to their discussion of DB2 projects, knowledge-based systems, and the client-server model applications with great interest. He sprinkled his conversation with amusing company stories about the early days of MIS and his work as a junior engineer. During the hour-and-a-half flight, a group seemed to form. A sense of adventure replaced the quiet intimidation with which the trip had begun.

The fourth day began with a regularly scheduled staff breakfast meeting and was followed by a final meeting on the restructuring presentation. The CIO reviewed the presentation at his desk again and had one overhead changed because of a syntax error. He reserved the time before the presentation at the Management Council meeting as quiet time. Following this important meeting were postmeeting reviews in the form of unscheduled meetings and a call.

The following morning, managers of all the Information Resource Organizations met for the first time as one group reporting to one manager. The day ended with a meeting on a group of young managers selected for a special leadership development program. The company's senior managers had developed a leadership profile which outlined "the behaviors, skills, and competencies" desired in company leaders.

Chronology Record

Almost 60% of the CIO's time was spent in meetings, 49% in scheduled meetings and 10% in unscheduled meetings (Appendix B.1). Thirty-four percent was spent on desk work.

Verbal Contacts

Although 44% of verbal contacts (Appendix B.2) were in the form of phone calls, 20% scheduled meetings, 25% unscheduled meetings, and 11% tours, 73% of contact time was spent in scheduled meetings but only 11% on phone calls. Meetings—scheduled and unscheduled—dominated verbal contacts (88% of contact time).

Seventy-one percent of participants and 62% of participant time was with subordinates; 10% of participants and 9% of participant time was with internal peers; 10% and 12% with suppliers/vendors; and 2% and 13% with independent or other. Four percent of contact time was with the CIO's two organizational superiors. With restructuring, the CIO would report to seven CEOs in what he called an inverted matrix and have nine direct reports. He had recommended having all IROs report to him but recommended that he, in turn, report to operating company CEOs. Restructuring would probably effect the distribution of participant contact time since working closely with each operating company CEO to affect changes in IRM was a leading objective for this change.

The CIO initiated 45% of all verbal contact time and the opposite party initiated 49%. The CIO spent 39% of contact time in his office, 25% in a conference or board room, and 25% away from the organization. During the week observed, 53% of contact time was for Mintzberg's purpose, "strategy," and 31% of time was for informational purposes.

The CIO met with smaller groups of people in over half of his scheduled meetings, almost 80% of his unscheduled meetings, and all of his tours involving one-on-one exchanges. For scheduled meetings, however, one third involved more than four people.

Incoming Mail

One third of incoming mail was periodicals or clippings (Appendix B.3). Since the company was publicly regulated and public opinion was influential, the CIO received news clippings mentioning the organization. He monitored business and financial periodicals and political events. Technology-related periodicals comprised 6% of his mail.

Reference data from inside the organization was the largest subcategory of incoming mail (21%). Examples of reference data from inside the organization were an Expert Systems Seminar schedule, the leadership profile, a fact sheet prepared for the CIO about participants in a luncheon he hosted, a message that an operating committee meeting had been canceled, and a summary of a staff meeting the CIO had not attended. Of the 21 pieces of mail in this category, 62% were received through the electronic mail system. This analysis offers some evidence to confirm the CIO's view that electronic mail opens communications channels and is one way to prevent the executive's isolation. Overall, 65% of all memos were electronic and 27% of all reports (Appendix D.3). Only the university CIO, who had also begun as a user of information technology instead of a data processing professional, received more electronic mail.

Outgoing Mail

Sixty percent of outgoing mail was in the form of a report. Preparation for the Management Council presentation was categorized as a report since the presentation would report back to the Council on restructuring alternatives. Mintzberg had no category for presentation preparation. Ten of the twelve report occurrences related to this presentation. One report was his leadership profile questionnaire and the other a questionnaire for a management association meeting. All but one memo was a response to incoming mail. Memos were 40% of outgoing mail. The CIO usually wrote a short memo on the piece or replied electronically immediately after reading an electronic mail message. He initiated fifty-five percent of his output. Clearly, however, this CIO did not use the written word as his primary means of communication. For the presentation report or overheads, he had described what he wanted to a subordinate and he edited the results. During the observation week, he did not spend time composing written communications. No letters were written, only short memos, two questionnaires, and the presentation report. However, he paid a writer's attention to syntax, grammar, and punctuation when editing the presentation overheads and handouts.

Half of the total targets for outgoing mail were superiors and internal peers. The remaining half were subordinates. Fifteen percent of outgoing mail was electronic. Output was dominated by the Management Council presentation report. In a conversation six weeks after the observation week, the CIO said that he had now devoted two months to restructuring and the provisions of restructuring. Therefore, he could not consider the desk work of the observation week atypical.

Activity Duration

Fifty-one percent of the CIO's activities consumed five minutes or less (Appendix B), with the heaviest grouping being at two and three minutes. Seventy-nine percent of activities lasted a half hour or less; almost 70% lasted 15 minutes or less.

Interaction Analysis

Half of verbal contacts time (Appendix H.7) was with the information technology unit and half outside the unit or with mixed groups. Fifty-nine percent of the mail involved areas other than the information technology unit: 40% involved external senders or targets and 19% was functional (Appendix D.1). The CIO's mail involving external participants was the highest of the CIOs observed. The 40% compares to 34, 33, 20, and 16%. Involvement with functional areas was the lowest at 19% compared to 38, 30, 27, and 22%. However, the interaction analysis of desk work and verbal contacts shows that this CIO is participating with all three groups.

Responsibility Analysis

Verbal Contacts

An analysis of verbal contacts by responsibility (Appendix E.1) shows that two of the eight responsibilities accounted for 93% of the utility CIO's time: strategic planning (73%), and coordination of the three groups (20%).

Desk Work

Forty percent of desk work was categorized as environmental scanning (Appendix E.2). The CIO scanned the political, utility, business/economic, and technological environment. Twenty-seven percent of pieces of mail involved the coordination of the three groups.

Verbal Contacts and Desk Work

On an occurrence basis for all verbal contacts and pieces of mail (Appendix E.3), coordination (28%), environmental scanning (23%), and strategic planning (21%) were primary responsibilities.

Roles Analysis

Verbal Contacts

The dominant role played during verbal contacts (Appendix F.1) was resource allocator (52% of time). Restructuring was categorized as resource allocation following Mintzberg's (1975) description of this role. The negotiator ranked second (16%). Informational roles were played 18% of the time and decisional roles, 74%. The leader role and liaison role were fairly equal (48%, 52%) (Appendix H.7).

Desk Work

Desk work was predominantly a monitoring activity for the utility CIO (Appendix F.5). Sixty-one percent of all mail was assigned this role, 70% of incoming and 20% of outgoing mail. Resource allocation ranked second. Informational roles were assigned to two thirds of the desk work. Although decisional roles dominated verbal contacts, informational roles dominated desk work. The leader role was played for about 40% of mail occurrences (Appendix D.1) and the liaison role, about 60%.

Verbal Contacts and Desk Work

All occurrences of contacts and pieces of mail (Appendix F.8) show informational roles assigned 49% percent of occurrences; decisional roles 43% and figurehead 8%.

10

Folklore and Facts Revisited

INTRODUCTION

Henry Mintzberg concluded his 1975 *Harvard Business Review* article, "The Manager's Job: Folklore and Fact," with this assertion: "No job is more vital to our society than that of the manager. The manager determines whether our social institutions will serve us well or whether they squander our talents and resources"(61). When this article was reprinted by the *Review* in March-April 1990 as a Management Classic, Mintzberg concluded his retrospective comments on the article with the same assertion (Mintzberg, 1990, 175). However, Mintzberg found managerial work to be largely misunderstood. He exposed four management folklores.

WHAT ARE THE FACTS FOR A CIO?

Each of Mintzberg's (1990) folklore and facts will be examined in terms of both a quantitative analysis of the data and from anecdotal data, observation notes, and conversations with the CIOs.

Planning

Perhaps the most important of Mintzberg's management facts was that managers, even CEOs, are not the planners described by management science. Instead, their work is hectic, fragmented, and biased toward action rather than reflection.

Meetings, particularly scheduled meetings, dominated the work day of both CEOs and CIOs. Despite the high number of activities observed—623 for

Table 10.1
Folklore and Fact

FOLKLORE	FACT
The manager is a reflective, systematic planner.	Study after study has shown that managers work at an unrelenting pace, that their activities are characterized by brevity, variety, and discontinuity, and that they are strongly oriented to action and dislike reflective activities (Mintzberg, 1990, 164).
The effective manager has no regular duties to perform.	Managerial work involves performing a number of regular duties, including ritual and ceremony, negotiations, and processing of soft information that links the organization with its environment (Mintzberg, 1990, 165).
The senior manager needs aggregated information, which a formal management information system best provides.	Managers strongly favor verbal media, telephone calls and meetings, over documents (Mintzberg, 1990, 165-66).
Management is, or at least is quickly becoming, a science and a profession.	The manager's programs—to schedule time, process information, make decisions, and so on—remain locked deep inside their brains (Mintzberg, 1990, 166-67).

CIOs and 547 for CEOs—attention for CIOs seemed divided into foreground and background activities. Each day, the CIO had an agenda of main events which made the flurry of activity coherent. Activities were related, and the observer did not sense fragmentation. Although the chronology records are not strikingly different (Appendix G.1), the conclusions reached using these coded data and observation notes are not the same as Mintzberg's. Mintzberg (1990, 164) concluded that

- "Managers work at an unrelenting pace"
- "Their activities are characterized by brevity, variety, and discontinuity"
- They are "strongly oriented to action"
- They "dislike reflective activities"
- They are not "reflective, systematic planners."

The activities of the CIOs observed were characterized by brevity and variety but not discontinuity. At the end of each day, the observer was able to sketch a "forest" view of the day and, likewise, for the week. The thrust of each CIO's activities emerged during the week.

At the insurance company, the CIO sought to heal wounds and build teamwork within the IT unit while establishing himself as a member of the inner circle of top management, a precarious and delicate task. At the university, the CIO likewise sought to integrate information technology into both academic and administrative life. To that effect, he sought alliances among academics and turned disturbance handling into an opportunity to effect a culture change. The manufacturing CIO found that the time had come to regroup and reconsider how the company deployed information technology. He labored over an IT architecture and uniform product pricing policy. Meanwhile, he worked with human and technological resources to do the best job possible now. In the government agency, a quiet commitment to a total quality approach was not overwhelmed by paperwork. Restructuring was the central theme at the utility company.

In short, these CIOs seemed to separate foreground and background activities effectively. Instead of being the victim of an unrelenting schedule, they seemed to expect this kind of schedule and were in control of their schedule to a large extent. They did not feel obligated to take every call or see every drop in visitor. None of the CIOs seemed to dislike reflective activities, although reflective activities often took place in meetings. Two CIOs sought out more reflective time with offices at home. The concentrated planning time needed to "work the tangible bits and pieces of information into a comprehensive picture" (Mintzberg, 1990, 174) was seized by these CIOs during the observation weeks. The comprehensive picture emerged from reflective activities, from desk work, and from the active habit of "reading situations," of mentally turning ongoing situations inside and out to discern motives and perceptions. These CIOs seem to follow Mintzberg's recommendation (1990, 175, 174):

The manager is challenged to gain control of his own time by turning obligations to his advantage . . . The manager is challenged to deal consciously with the pressures of superficiality by giving serious attention to the issues that require it, by stepping back in order to see a broad picture.

While CIOs did have desk work sessions of longer duration, the broad picture or thrust of their activities was not the result of reflection as much as interactions which constantly told them the shape of things. In fact, reading situations accurately seemed more important than planning the details of implementation.

The manufacturing CIO commented that seeing things the way they really are "eyeball to eyeball without flinching" or denying what he saw was the most difficult and important part of his job. For example, he had to face the fact that deploying information technology in the field, with agents, was becoming a precarious strategy and not be defensive about criticism because of his personal involvement in this strategy. The insurance company CIO had to recognize the distrust among the information technology unit as a result of restructuring and the resignation of the previous CIO. He had to recognize the political implications of his position as information technology became a critical element in the company's strategy. He worked to have senior management invite him to be a peer and promote him. Although he subscribed to *CIO* magazine, he carefully avoided the use of the term.

The university CIO realized that the culture change he needed to effect could not be attacked head on without loss of support. Instead, he used indirect methods:

- A study at another university which he would publish at his university for his two superiors as well
- A good project skillfully played as a foil for a project gone awry because it was typical of the old way of doing things
- Acquisition of increased control over information resource planning by gaining approval for a new computer fee
- Seizing approval responsibility for how the fee revenue will be used.

In the government agency, the CIO was a practiced reader of situations involving contractors. He sensed that a contractor had asked for an unauthorized taping of a videoconference about its contract. Because he had agency-wide responsibility, he often used phone contacts to probe the reactions of key people to various events or correspondence.

In the utility company, the CIO knew whose support could be gained by giving them all the information they wanted and whose support could not be gained in this way. In fact, communication would simply better arm them to oppose him. He realized that the opposition was not personal and clearly perceived business reasons for opposing the plan. He also understood that "right sizing" had made everyone justifiably uneasy about their future, so turf protection would be an important factor.

Reading the situation was part of the problem definition process and was not accomplished entirely through reflective or analytical desk work. Instead, reading the situation was more a habit of mind, a way of thinking and experiencing. The use of metaphor and analogy seemed to be associated with this reading of situations.

All five CIOs observed used analogies, some more frequently than others. The university CIO told the observer that a fellow university CIO believed the ability to construct analogies was a critical success factor for CIOs, a critical bridge-building activity. With analogies, CIOs were able to grasp the essence of a situation and pass the message along in an immediately understandable way. The utility CIO told a subordinate that well-timed incremental restructuring changes were like feeding farm animals: "We don't want to put the whole bale out at once, just one meal at a time." The manufacturing CIO used the powerful analogy of "a baby in an iron lung" and many others. The insurance company CIO had developed an elaborate analogy of the move to the new data center with uninterrupted services to World War II and even assigned senior executives the roles of war heroes—Marshall, Ike, Patton, and President Roosevelt. The government agency CIO at a weekly staff meeting gave the analogy of Joseph negotiating for the Israelites in Egypt. The Egyptians continued to quibble over details, so Joseph offered them more than they were asking for to end negotiations and reach a settlement. In a meeting about the human resource system, the university CIO told a participant, "We can't do fishes and loaves, Don. If the new system requires more, you're understaffed." He tells them that conversion to the new system will be difficult: "When a new road is opened up, there's traffic problems for months." The CIOs used analogies to communicate the situation as they read it and to shape how others read the situation.

So while activities were brief, 50% were seven minutes or less compared to nine minutes for Mintzberg and activities were varied, activities were not characterized by discontinuity. A change in activity (i.e., a change in communication medium and/or participant) did not equate to a mental shift or shift in focus. Important issues, like a recurring musical theme in a symphony, emerged quickly and provided both continuity and coherence. CIOs were not so much victimized by "work at an unrelenting pace . . . characterized by brevity, variety, and discontinuity" (Mintzberg 1990, 164) but active participants, continually reading and shaping events as well as the perception of events and providing continuity in the work day and week.

Unlike the CEOs observed, the CIOs observed did not seem to dislike reflective activities. Desk work sessions were longer (29 minutes versus 15), and a higher percentage of time was spent on desk work. However, much of the managers' reflective activity was concurrent with other activities. Discussions at scheduled and unscheduled meetings furthered thinking as well. In fact, 35% of verbal contacts were used for strategic planning compared to only 9% of desk work. Scheduled meetings, which comprised two thirds of verbal contact time, did have longer durations—59 minutes on average, twice the length of average desk work sessions. Although the CIOs were infrequently reflective, systematic planners in the management science sense, the CIOs were not simply responding to the pressures of their job. Instead, they actively sought to read their situations, had coherent agendas, and were constantly shaping events toward those agendas. Reflection and planning were an ongoing process, not an isolated, desk work activity.

This study found the five CIOs to be planners, but planners who realized the difficulty of reading the present situation and thus effectively changing the situation. Planning was most often an interactive, team activity rather than a solitary activity. However, two CIOs sought out the sedentary, reflective time Mintzberg refers to by using home offices, two arrived an hour or so before the normal work day to have a quiet hour, and one used lunch at his desk as a quiet hour.

CIOs did work at an unrelenting pace; their activities were characterized by brevity and variety but also by a remarkable continuity or coherence, controlled by an agenda. They had a bias for action (spending 72% of their time in verbal communication compared to 78% for Mintzberg's CEOs) but did not dislike reflective activities and were often able to do both at the same time, actively reading the situations in which they participated.

Mintzberg's first fact of managerial work was that managers work at an unrelenting pace, which prevents them from being "reflective, systematic planners":

The chief executives met a steady stream of callers and mail from the moment they arrived in the morning until they left in the evening. Coffee breaks and lunches were inevitably work related, and ever-present subordinates seemed to usurp any free moment. (1990, 164)

While the situation described by Mintzberg fit the CIO experience, the work pace, "steady stream of callers" and "ever present subordinates" were largely initiated and orchestrated by the CIOs. They were not the victim of this pace, nor were they simply reacting to it. These CIOs initiated half of their verbal contacts; 10% were regularly scheduled events and only the remaining 40% were initiated by others. Not only did they set the work pace, but they also chose which subordinates had access to them. Even requests for unscheduled meetings and phone calls were filtered through administrative assistants or secretaries. If questionable, the CIO made the decision to participate or not in the contact.

Further, as noted previously, two CIOs sometimes worked at home in the early morning and evenings, isolated from this steady stream of contacts and two came in early before the stream began. Coffee breaks were not taken but coffee or other beverages was consumed during meetings or while otherwise working. One CIO ate lunch at his desk or during meetings; another used lunch for travel time, desk work, and a business luncheon; one had an "office" table at a local restaurant, and one used lunch to exercise in the faculty fitness center in order to maintain faculty contacts. However, there was no sense of subordinates usurping time. CIOs seemed comfortable with the work pace and even thrived on it.

Both CEOs and CIOs spent close to half of participant time with subordinates.

CIOs and CEOs spent between 7 and 8% of their contact time with their superior—a Director-level person for the CEO and a Vice President, President, or CEO-level person for the CIO. Alliances with internal peers was critical for CIOs. The CEOs, on the other hand, spent more of their peer contact time with external peers, since they had no internal peers.

Mintzberg (1968, 188) grouped his verbal contact purpose categories along a continuum of active and passive purposes as a "means of assessing the manager's degree of self-control." This continuum is duplicated here and shows the CEOs and the CIOs proportion of contact occurrences along this continuum.

	CEO	CIO
PASSIVE	42%	27%
Status requests, solicitations		
Authority and action requests		
Ceremony		
Receiving information		
NEUTRAL	27%	33%
Review		
Scheduling		
External board work		
ACTIVE	31%	40%
Strategy		
Negotiation		
Giving information		
Touring		
Manager requests		

Mintzberg (1968, 188) acknowledged that this chart was a "crude" indicator of the "extent of self control" but concluded that since 42% of verbal contacts were on the passive side of the continuum and 31% on the active, "the manager appears to control fewer activities than do those around him." The CIOs observed, on the other hand, were on the passive side of Mintzberg's continuum for 27% of contacts and on the active side for 40%.

Some further conclusions about the CIO's work can be reached as a result of the quantitative analysis of verbal contact subcategories and these conclusions can be compared to Mintzberg's (1990, 164-65) conclusions regarding the folklore of managers' being "reflective, systematic planners":

When managers must plan, they seem to do so implicitly in the context of daily actions, not in some abstract process reserved for two weeks in the organization's mountain retreat. The plans of the chief executives I studied seemed to exist only in their heads—as flexible, but often specific, intentions. The traditional literature notwithstanding, the job of managing does not breed reflective planners; managers respond to stimuli, they are conditioned by their jobs to prefer live to delayed action.

The CIOs observed did not attend a two-week mountain retreat, but their strategic planning was not just in the context of daily action or operational planning. Open-ended sessions were a significant activity, consuming more time than operational planning. Furthermore, written summaries documenting the discussions and conclusions of these meetings were issued. In one of the two organizations in which this type of meeting was not held, the CIO's major written output was a summary from an open-ended strategic planning session held the previous week. This manufacturing CIO called himself the scribe because he always volunteered for this documentation of senior executive meetings. In the other of the two organizations that did not hold open-ended strategic planning sessions, the university President, who would have attended open-ended strategy sessions, was unavailable for meetings that week due to an unanticipated public relations crisis.

CIOs observed were real time responders with a fourth of all verbal contacts requiring a real-time response (instant communications—4%; responding to requests for authorization—5%, or information—2%, or influencing pressures—3%; status requests or solicitations—3%; giving information on plans and policies—5%; and giving advice—3%). However, the one delayed action task of open-ended strategy session by itself consumed 13% of contact time. Considering the documentation and editing which followed such sessions, one could not conclude from the CIOs observed that the "job of managing does not breed reflective planners" (Mintzberg, 1990, 165). Since these sessions typically involved the senior management group, this statement could also apply to other executives. CIOs were real time responders, but these activities did not preclude verbal participation in delayed-action activities or planning. They were more like skilled jugglers than systematic planners, however. Planning was part of their work process, not an isolated activity.

Media for Information

Another of Mintzberg's (1990, 165-66) folklore and facts relates to the first one considered. Mintzberg found that managers shun the use of written information and favor word of mouth:

Folklore: The senior manager needs aggregated information, which a formal management information system best provides.
Fact: Managers strongly favor the verbal media—namely, telephone calls and meetings.

The fact was that CIOs spent more time in the verbal mediums because of the dominance of scheduled meetings. Nevertheless, CIOs observed found the written medium an important one. We could not conclude that they favor the verbal media, but instead they use the written media and reports from management information systems in a different way. Both incoming and outgoing mail were examined in this regard.

Incoming Mail

Mintzberg observed 659 pieces of incoming mail; the CIO study observed 355 pieces. Letters and reports accounted for over half the mail for the CEOs observed in 1968. For the CIOs observed in 1990, the memo form alone accounted for almost half of the 355 pieces of incoming mail. Mintzberg (1990, 166) concluded that "not much of the mail provides "live current information" and reported that the five CEOs treat mail as "a burden to be dispensed with," coming in on Saturday morning to process 142 pieces of mail in just over three hours, to get rid of all the stuff, in his words. Mintzberg also concluded that "the computer . . . has apparently had no influences on the work procedures of general managers" (1990, 167).

Table 10.2
Incoming Mail Analysis

FORM	CIOs	CEOs
Letter	17%	38%
Memo	46%	16%
Report	17%	25%
Periodical	15%	16%
Clipping	4%	4%
Book	1%	1%

CIOs had responded to the problem of useless mail by having the mail they received filtered by a skilled administrative assistant or secretary. In three cases, this filtered mail was organized into folders. Furthermore, the computer had an influence on work procedures. Checking the electronic mail was one of the first tasks performed by four of the five CIOs. A third of all memos were electronic. Electronic mail was current and timely. If electronic mail had been ignored until Saturday, meetings would have been missed. One fourth of all the mail was electronic. One CIO did not use electronic mail but relied on fax machines. Another used an Executive Support System and checked reports from this system routinely each morning.

Electronic mail and voice mail made the CIOs accessible to timely information without having to be available always. According to Mintzberg (1990, 166), "the manager who misses the telephone call revealing that the company's biggest customer was seen golfing with his main competitor may read about a dramatic drop in sales in the next quarterly report." The CIOs observed did not have to be available constantly to keep current.

An analysis of the CIOs' desk work shows the CIO accepting or approving of new policies and resource commitments, new programs and procedures, and exceptions to normal policies and procedures. A wide variety of internal reference information is skimmed. Reports on operations and general reports are both regular and ad hoc. Overall, incoming mail was not a "burden to be dispensed with" but an essential function of relatively high interest to the CIOs. Because the CIOs' mail was filtered, they did not get rid of much stuff.

Outgoing Mail

CIOs generated less than half the outgoing mail of CEOs, 109 pieces versus 231 for CEOs in 215 and 202 observation hours, respectively. Output as a percent of input was closer, however: 31% for CIOs and 35% for CEOs. The CIOs were less reactive, however, initiating two thirds of their output and responding to input about one third of the time. CEOs, on the other hand, initiated only a tenth of outgoing mail, responding to incoming mail about 90% of the time.

Initiation of written communication is one evidence of the importance of the written medium to CIOs, as is the organizational importance of the chief single purpose for incoming mail: resource, policy, and procedure decisions. Mail did provide live, current information, especially electronic and fax mail. Mail processing did not seem a burden, not only because the total volume was almost half that of CEOs (464 total pieces versus 890 for CEOs) but also because it had been processed, filtered, organized, and marked before the CIO saw the incoming mail. Formal management information systems were used for regular periodic reports. However, about half the reports—both operational and general—were customized or upon request, ad hoc rather than routinely generated. These reports were qualitative as well as quantitative, with report providers using microcomputer applications such as spreadsheets to generate special analyses and graphics.

Qualitative evidence of the importance of the written media is that the strategic planning meetings were placed in written form. One CIO asked on a job profile about the importance of written communication to his job, answered, "Important!" Another met with technical writers to review and revise an information resource policy document. The written medium dominated the time of the university CIO. The utility CIO analyzed the wording of a report carefully commenting on the power of using *common* versus *centralized* to describe certain systems which all operating companies would share.

There are many alternative explanations for this difference in written mediums and use of reports, and valid conclusions about CEOs versus CIOs could not be drawn. However, the five CIOs observed used and valued the written medium. They used the written medium for organizational decision making and current, live information. They realized the long-lasting effect, especially in the strategy and policy area, of a written shaping of plans, policies, and procedures. They did not find decisions on a choice of words trivial.

Regular Duties

Another of Mintzberg's folklores was that effective managers have no regular duties. The fact that he (1990, 165) observed was that "Managerial work involves performing a number of regular duties, including ritual and ceremony, negotiations, and processing of soft information that links the organization to its environment." For CIOs, regularly scheduled verbal contacts were only 2% of total contacts, compared to 7% for CEOs. Ceremony was 2% of CEOs' contact time, compared to 5% for CIOs. About half the CIOs' reports were regularly scheduled. In fact, because schedules were not regular or fixed, keeping the calendar correct and scheduling events required 13% of contact occurrences, compared to 15% for CEOS.

CIOs had few regular or routine duties, especially with regard to verbal contacts. Verbal contacts were for the purpose of strategy and information exchange (receiving and giving information, review) over three fourths of the time. Desk work, on the other hand, did involve certain routine, regular duties. The main purpose of desk work was authority requests or authorizations. Signature folders and red folders were organized for this duty. For CIOs, managerial work involved performing few regular duties, the chief of which was approval of resource commitments and policy.

Handling exceptions was not the CIO's expectation for the day's work. Each had a proactive agenda that provided an overriding purpose in the context of which other actions made sense. The stability of the organizational or external environment was not such that the CIO could merely handle exceptions to present polices or procedures. Instead, approving new policies occurred more than the subcategory of exception to normal procedures (76% versus 4%).

For CIOs observed, regular duties are more a characteristic of desk work than verbal contacts. The CIO pursues an agenda, which changes over time. In addition to this agenda, he participates in strategy formulation. He keeps informed through verbal and written exchanges of information. Authority requests, a regular duty, are largely desk work or written.

Management as a Science

Mintzberg's (1990, 166-67) last folklore is one indicator of the difference in the beliefs about management in 1968 and the 1990s: "Management is, or at least is quickly becoming, a science and a profession." According to Mintzberg (1990, 166), "a science involves the enaction of systematic, analytically determined procedures or programs." The fact he observed was that "the managers' programs—to schedule time, process information, make decisions, and so on—remain locked deep inside their brains." Mintzberg continued,

I was struck during my study by the fact that the executives I was observing—all very competent—are fundamentally indistinguishable from their counterparts of a hundred years ago (or a thousand years ago). The information they need differs, but they seek it in the same way—by word of mouth. Their decisions concern modern technology, but the procedures they use to make those decisions are the same as the procedures of the nineteenth-century manager.

CIOs observed did use the new tools of information technology, and this use seemed to extend availability beyond verbal contacts. Managing was a complex task, involving interpersonal, organizational, and environmental considerations which shifted or changed frequently. The certainty which would allow the "inaction of systematic, analytically determined procedures or programs" (Mintzberg, 1990, 166) did not seem present. Instead, CIOs pursued their changing agendas with great sensitivity to timing, interpersonal relationships, organizational politics, and the business environment. Each realized the power of figurative language. For critical policy and strategy decisions, each organization placed the decision in written form. An observation of five successful CIOs leads one to the conclusion that many of the so-called soft arts which prepare students to excel in communications skills and to deal with nuance and ambiguity would be a valuable partner to the hard analysis of management science.

11

Managerial Roles

MINTZBERG'S ROLES FRAMEWORK

The day-to-day activities observed by Mintzberg while shadowing CEOs bore little resemblance to Fayol's (Mintzberg 1990) classic description of managerial work: planning, organizing, controlling. Managerial work was much more dynamic and complex. Understandably, several years later he borrowed a metaphor from drama to describe managerial work. Managers play certain roles, and these roles are influenced by their situation and rank within the organization. These roles overlap and may be played simultaneously. Managing is a tenuous task. These 10 roles were described in Chapter 4.

Mintzberg emphasized that these roles form a gestalt, an integrated whole. All 10 roles must be considered together. However, "to say that the ten roles form a gestalt is not to say that all managers give equal attention to each role. In fact, I found in my review of the various research studies that . . . staff managers spend the most time in the informational roles, since they are experts who manage departments and advise other parts of the organization" (Mintzberg 1990, 172-73).

CIOs did not fit the mold for a staff manager, with only 36% of all verbal contacts and pieces of mail in the informational roles and 60% in the decisional. The remaining 4% of occurrences were in the interpersonal role of figurehead, during which the CIO performed ceremonial duties with little informational or decisional impact.

The leader role within the CIOs' unit accounted for 49% of all occurrences and the liaison role accounted for 47% of all occurrences. Mintzberg's CEOs averaged 44% of their time on liaison activities (Mintzberg 1990, 169). For 4% of occurrences, both leader and liaison roles were played because participants involved those inside and outside the vertical chain of command.

On an occurrence basis, the resource allocator and monitoring roles were dominant, followed by disturbance handling. However, when percentage of time spent playing each role is considered (as it can be for verbal contacts, which represent 72% of the observation time for CIOs), resource allocator, entrepreneur, and disturbance handler were the most time consuming and monitoring ranked fourth.

Roles and Medium Employed

Roles were further analyzed by mediums used to determine whether CIOs tended to use certain mediums to play certain roles. Monitoring was largely an incoming mail activity with a fairly even distribution for other mediums. Mintzberg's (1973, 58) observation that "a good part of the information the manager collects in his monitor role arrives in verbal form, often as gossip, hearsay, and speculation" does not hold for CIOs. This kind of information may be more important but does not consume more time or account for more occurrences. The spokesperson role, informing and satisfying "the influential people who control his organizational unit" (Mintzberg 1990, 171), was characteristically an outgoing mail activity.

The entrepreneurial role, critical to the CIO's participation in strategic planning, was identified with scheduled meetings and outgoing mail, which often documented these meetings. Disturbance handling was a verbal contact task, with calls and unscheduled meetings dominating, as would be expected since "the disturbance handler role depicts the manager involuntarily responding to pressures. Here change is beyond the manager's control. The pressures of the situation are too severe to be ignored" (Mintzberg 1990, 171). The major role played, resource allocator, was distributed across all mediums, ranking first for scheduled meetings, unscheduled meetings, calls, and incoming desk work and ranking second for outgoing desk work, behind entrepreneurial activities.

The remaining roles—figurehead, disseminator, and negotiator—are difficult to characterize by medium except to say that figurehead is most characteristically a meeting activity, scheduled and unscheduled, and negotiation is a verbal contact activity that requires preparation, and thus is characteristically scheduled rather than unscheduled meetings and calls. The disseminator role, the passing of information within the CIO's work unit, employs the verbal contact mediums fairly evenly but, as would be expected, is primarily an outgoing mail activity.

Decisional roles dominated the verbal contact mediums (69%), but information and decisional roles were more evenly distributed for mail. Three fourths of all scheduled meetings required decisional roles and these roles were chiefly resource allocator and entrepreneur. Almost two thirds of all unscheduled meetings were characterized as decisional roles, chiefly resource allocator and disturbance handler. Calls resembled scheduled meetings in that three fourths primary role was were decisional and the resource allocator. As with unscheduled meetings, however, disturbance handling replaced entrepreneur as the

Table 11.1
Characteristic Mediums for Roles

Figurehead	meetings
Monitor	incoming mail
Disseminator	outgoing mail
Spokesman	outgoing mail
Entrepreneur	scheduled meetings, outgoing mail
Disturbance handler	calls, unscheduled meetings
Resource Allocator	all mediums
Negotiator	scheduled meetings and calls

second major role. Incoming desk work is characterized by resource allocator and monitoring, whereas outgoing desk work can be characterized by entrepreneur, resource allocator, spokesman, and disseminator.

Variation in Roles Played

Some roles were played more frequently by one CIO than by others. General conclusions, considering exceptions, from an examination of this pattern are as follows:

- The utility CIO played the monitoring, figurehead, and negotiating roles more frequently, but played the disturbance-handling role least frequently.

- The government agency and manufacturing CIO played the resource allocation role more frequently. However, even without these higher frequencies, the resource allocation role was played most frequently by the five CIOs.

- The university CIO played the disturbance-handling role more frequently, but disturbance handling remains the third most frequently played role even with this exception.

The overall pattern of roles which emerges is as follows:

Rank	Role
(by occurrence frequency)	
1	Resource allocator
2	Monitor

3   Disturbance handler
4   Entrepreneur, spokesperson, disseminator
5   Figurehead
6   Negotiator

Entrepreneurial activity was time consuming, and its percentage was higher on a time basis than on an occurrence basis. For verbal contacts, the time spent playing each role was ranked:

Time
Rank	Role
1	Resource allocator
2	Entrepreneur, Disturbance handler
3	Monitor, Disseminator
4	Figurehead, Negotiator, Spokesman

Resource allocation was the only role in which all CIOs spent more than 10% of verbal time. All but one spent more than 20% of verbal time on resource allocation.

The Resource Allocation Role

The analysis of activities by Mintzberg's role framework shows the interrelatedness of roles and the ambiguity of the coding decisions. However, the analysis leads to an important finding with regard to CIOs: the overriding importance of the resource allocator role. According to Mintzberg (1990, 172), "The manager is responsible for deciding who will get what." For the CIO, the resource allocator role went beyond the information technology unit to the allocation of information technology resources throughout the organization.

Mintzberg (1990, 172) comments that "Perhaps the most important resource the manager allocates is his or her own time." Scheduling was a constant activity, and administrative assistants guarded the CIO's time not only by guarding access but also by filtering and organizing mail. Travel time was planned and used by CIOs. Those organizations that owned a company plane provided that plane's use for the CIO.

Mintzberg (1990, 172) describes the resource allocator role as the one in which "The manager is also charged with designing the unit's structure, that pattern of formal relationships that determines how work is to be divided and coordinated." The work units of all CIOs observed had undergone a major restructuring within two years or were undergoing restructuring at present. The insurance CIO's unit had been downsized and reorganized from a project structure to a process structure in which analysis, design, and implementation were in different work groups. At the university, academic and administrative computing as well as telecommunications had been placed in one new Information Technology Division, with administrative computing no longer reporting to Finance. The manufacturing CIO had downsized, combining field support and internal support functions. In the government agency, telecommunications and computing had been combined into an Information Systems Division. The utility CIO was in the midst of a major restructuring following a "right sizing" of the entire organization, including the consolidation of data centers.

Mintzberg (1990, 172) emphasizes the strategic importance of the resource allocator:

Also, in his role as resource allocator, the manager authorizes the important decisions of his unit before they are implemented. By retaining this power, the manager can insure that decisions are interrelated. To fragment this power is to encourage discontinuous decision making and a disjointed strategy.

All CIOs observed participated in strategic planning to varying degrees and thus were prepared to make decisions regarding information technology in light of that strategy. The government agency CIO participated in strategy to a lesser degree, and the disjointed nature of the agency with its project teams, multiple sites, and contractors did not lend itself to a unifying strategy. Resource allocation was a major task for him, however, and was a means of exerting influence in an area of importance to him—software standards and efficient access to the network. The university CIO planned to leverage the resource allocation role, using the new computer fees to integrate further academic and administrative computing and to influence both. The utility CIO's restructuring would channel all information technology resource approvals through him, not just for the services company which housed the major Information Resource Organization but for all operating companies as well. The organization had decided that this channeling was critical to its strategy to be competitive in a nonregulated environment. The manufacturing CIO had made information technology resource decisions over the years and thus a widespread, diverse agent network could operate with the organization's product divisions. Because he approved acquisition, an architecture, One Lilbourne Architecture or OLA, could be implemented; and this architecture provided strategic advantages. The insurance company CIO's recommendations carried a great deal of weight, as evidenced by the recent allocation of funds to a new data center. He actively sought ways to add value by using present resources and acquiring others, such as image processing software.

Resource allocation tasks were given priority, and three of five CIOs had them grouped into signature folders and processed these folders daily. Mintzberg (1990, 172) observed that "executives in my study made a great many authorizations decisions on an ad hoc basis. Apparently, many projects cannot wait or simply do not have the quantifiable costs and benefits that capital budgeting requires."

The CIOs observed budgeted general amounts for anticipated and unanticipated projects but approved specific, nonroutine projects, considering the effect on the budgeted amount. A procedure for acquisition existed, even for smaller information technology purchases such as microcomputers. Administrative assistants checked all proposals for appropriate information and accuracy. Only one major ad hoc decision without formal consideration of "quantifiable costs and benefits" was made, and that occurred when a crisis at the manufacturing company precipitated a rather quick remedy as a business necessity. Time and personnel, on the other hand, as well as expense monies were often allocated on an ad hoc basis as adjustments to changing conditions.

Mintzberg (1990,172) observed that "One common solution to approving projects is to pick the person instead of the proposal." For ad hoc decisions, this may have been the case with CIOs. The observer could not make this determination. However, with larger projects, particularly with capital projects, the first determination was the fit of the project with organizational strategy. In the manufacturing company, where the strategy was to present one face to the market, the fit of the project within the architecture was critical. In the insurance company, which sought to cut costs and add value, image processing offered both. In the utility company, information technology solutions common to all operating companies but still allowing for customization were being sought. Therefore, database projects using cooperative processing were being funded. At the university, where a computer-intensive academic environment for faculty and students was an overriding strategic objective, funding for faculty and student information technology had been accelerated and a new source of funds applied to these projects.

A resource dilemma for CIOs was assigning the right person to these major projects instead of picking the person and then the project. In the utility company, insurance company, and university, major database projects were assigned to "rising stars" so that their expertise in this area could be honed. In the manufacturing company, finding the right person for several demanding projects was a dilemma. A source of constant frustration for the government agency CIO was the required consideration of extraneous factors before a person could be selected. A case in point was a telecommunications engineer for the videoconferencing project. This person had to meet Equal Opportunity Commission (EOC) guidelines and not fall outside certain civil service salary ranges.

12

Comparison with Ives and Olson's MIS Managers

INTRODUCTION

Ives and Olson (1981) employed the structured observation methodology and, to a large extent, Mintzberg's coding for a study of six MIS managers for three to four days each from four industry types. Three of six managers observed were from manufacturing companies. Ives and Olson (1981) did not analyze pieces of mail. However, they coded message units to determine whether the content of communication was more technical or managerial.

LIMITATIONS OF BOTH STUDIES

Ives and Olson (1981, 60) cite the limitations of their study:

it is based on a small, self-selected sample of managers that may not be representative of the broader population . . . [and] we provided some methodological rigor through the structured observation approach. . . . Nevertheless, this type of study is, almost by definition, nonrigorous. It provides us with a rather fuzzy, big picture of the information systems manager's job.

Of course, this statement applies to the CIO study as well, especially in regard to those coding elements which were judgmental: purposes, roles, and responsibilities. These elements provide some cross check to anecdotal evidence from 25 days of observation. However, other coding elements were not judgmental: activity changes, mediums, durations, participants, forms of correspondence, location, and group membership for participants.

Results may not be representative, however. In the CIO study, selection was made after research to qualify the CIO according to Brumm's (1988b) operational definition, and selection was made across industry types. Scheduled meeting percentages were compared with a month's calendar and both CIO and administrative assistants questioned about how typical the week was. Furthermore, the titles, reporting relationships, and profile for the five CIOs were compared to the profile for the 111 CIOs from *Fortune* 100 Service and Fortune 100 Industrial companies participating in Brumm's survey (1988b). From this evidence, one cannot conclude that the CIOs or observation weeks were repre-

Table 12.1
Comparison of Brumm's (1988a, 1988b) Fortune 100 Survey
Participants and Five CIOs Observed

Profile	Fortune 100	Observed
Hours/week	56	44
Average age	50	54
Race	white	white
Sex	male	male
Marital status	married	married
Birthplace	U.S	U.S.
Avg. years formal schooling	17	19
Percent business related degrees	59%	60%
Employment Background DP/MIS	8%	60%
Hired from within for position	72%	80%
Years in current position	3	3.6
Vice President	36%	40%
Senior Vice President	17%	0%
Director	16%	20%
Executive VP	8%	-
Other titles	23%	-
Reporting Relations		
-by titles		
Chairman, CEO, COO,President	31%	40%
Executive Vice President	21%	40%
Vice President	14%	-
Senior Vice President	14%	-
Vice Chairman	8%	-
Others	12%	20%
-by function		
Independent of function	50%	80%
Financial	25%	-
Administrative	6%	20%
Other	19%	-

sentative, but the evidence suggests that CIOs were not unrepresentative. Major differences are that the five CIOs observed did work 12 less hours per week on average than was reported by the 111 CIOs, and reported at a higher level within their organizations, and none reported to Finance. Their personal, education, and employment profiles were similar to the average for Brumm's survey (1988b).

WORK CHARACTERISTICS

Number of Activities

Ives and Olson (1981, 53) note that "previous research has shown that lower level managers are involved in more activities per day, each of shorter duration, than managers in positions of greater authority." The number of activities performed in this study is consistent with these findings. The total number of activities averaged per day was 46 for MIS managers, 22 for CEOs, and 25 for CIOs. The range for MIS managers was 28 to 63; for CEOs, 19 to 32; for CIOs, 19 to 30.

Duration of Activities

The average duration of activities for MIS managers was 13 minutes; for CEOs, 22 minutes; and for CIOs, 22 minutes. Seventy percent of MIS managers' activities lasted less than nine minutes compared to about half of CEO and CIO activities (49% for CEOs and 54% for CIOs). Only 2% of MIS managers' activities lasted longer than an hour compared to 9% for CEOs and 10% for CIOs. Mason's (1984, 144) study of staff information managers showed that these staff specialists, like the MIS managers, averaged only 2% of activities lasting longer than one hour.

Duration of Activities within Communication Mediums

Within mediums, differences are less distinct (Appendix H.2 compares the mediums used by Mintzberg's CEOs, Ives and Olson's MIS managers, and the CIOs discussed in this book). Certainly, the broad picture provided by the aforementioned comparison is that CIOs' work characteristics more closely resemble those of an executive than an MIS manager, and those of a general manager than a staff specialist. The executive status goes further than reporting position within the organization. Work characteristics are those found by other studies to be associated with executive-level work.

An exceptional area for CIOs was desk work sessions. The CIOs had longer average desk work sessions, 29 minutes compared to 15 for CEOs and 9 for MIS managers. Although two CIOs were within the range Mintzberg observed for CEOs (12 to 20 minutes), all others exceeded the range for CEOs. On the other hand, none of the MIS managers were even within the lower level for CIOs, 16 minutes. The longest average desk work session duration for any individual MIS managers was 13 minutes.

Phone calls averaged six minutes for CEOs and CIOs but four minutes for MIS managers. Scheduled meetings averaged 68 minutes for CEOs, 59 for CIOs, and 40 for MIS managers. When these durations by communication mediums are compared with Mason's staff specialists results, the groupings tend to be CEO and CIO, MIS manager and staff specialist. In fact, Mason (1984, 144) concluded that "other studies of functional managers . . . (Ives and Olson 1981) . . . are most comparable to those of this study [staff specialist]."

An overview of total time spent by communication mediums shows that all managers spent most of their time in scheduled meetings: CEOs, 59% of their time; CIOs and MIS managers, 48% of their time. Unscheduled meetings consumed 20% of MIS managers' time, 10% of CEOs' time, and 14% of CIOs' time. MIS managers spent 19% of their time on desk work; CEOs, 22%; and CIOs, 28%. CIOs spent more time in the written mediums and had longer desk work sessions on average than both CEOs and MIS managers.

Location of Activities

Rosemary Stewart (1976) found that staff managers tend to remain within their own territory. McCall's (1978) summary of work studies indicated that the percent of time spent outside the manager's office increased with rank. This finding was confirmed in the Ives and Olson study (1981, 54), where 58% of the verbal contacts were in the manager's office and 26% in a conference room or board room. The MIS managers were away from their own office or a conference room only 15% of their contact time (Appendix H.3). This per-centage compares to 47% for CEOs and 40% for CIOs observed. CEOs were in their office 39% of contact time and CIOs 33% of contact time. Both CEOs and CIOs spent significant contact time away from the organization, 38% and 27%, respectively. MIS mangers spent only 6% of contact time away from their organizations.

Initiation of Contacts

The number of activities, duration of activities, and location of activities align the CIO with the executive role. Proportion of time spent among mediums is less consistent, with the CIO resembling neither in desk work, resembling the MIS manager with proportion of time in scheduled meetings and phone calls, and resembling the CEO in proportion of time in unscheduled meetings. CIOs were not like MIS managers in terms of the percent of contacts initiated by the manager. CEOs initiated the contact, or the contact was mutual only 37% of the time compared to 58% for both MIS managers and CIOs.

Activity Participants

In scheduled meetings, CIOs had fewer one-on-one meetings (39%) than either MIS managers (53%) or CEOs (44%). CIOs attended a higher percentage of scheduled meetings with more than four people: 45% compared to 34% for CEOs and 27% for MIS managers. Although the percentage of total time in scheduled meetings was the same for MIS managers, CIOs' meetings tended to last longer and involve more people. CEOs spent 48% of their contact time with subordinates and CIOs spent 49%. However, MIS managers spent 61% of their contact time with subordinates.

Manager or Technician?

According to Ives and Olson (1981, 50), their research was motivated by four "underlying concerns":

- "What are the relative contributions of technical and managerial expertise required of the information systems manager?"
- "What does this person do all day?"
- "What is the "role of the information systems manager as a communications link with the rest of the organization . . . and other organizations?"
- "What is the set of problems facing information systems management that could benefit from future research?"

They did not use purpose categories but instead analyzed message units seeking answers to their research questions. Their analysis of 7459 message units showed that only 3% of the MIS managers' message units and 5% of other participants' message units were technical, "those felt to be difficult for a person with no technical expertise (i.e., related to information systems) to understand" (Ives and Olson 1981, 55). The subjects of message units were 43% general management, 8% software, 11% operations, and 7% hardware. Ives and Olson concluded that the MIS manager's role was managerial rather than technical. "Good technical support from subordinates replaces much of the manager's need for 'hands-on' technical skills" (Ives and Olson 1981, 61). Although message units were not used to observe CIOs, anecdotal evidence and interaction patterns suggests that the same conclusion would apply to CIOs.

Communication Link

However, Ives and Olson (1981, 61) found the MIS manager as a communication link problematic: "One can conclude that the contact of information system managers with functional management at their own level is noticeably absent." Indeed, a grouping of participants by those outside the MIS manager's line of responsibility shows that 39% of verbal contact time was outside the unit and 61% inside the unit. For CIOs, 58% of contact time was outside the information technology unit and 42% within. The CIOs' verbal interaction outside the unit was distributed among other functional units, external participants, and a combination of those outside along with those inside the unit. An analysis of mail also shows a similar pattern for CIOs. More occurrences of mail involved senders and targets outside the information technology unit than from within it. The range of contact time outside the information technology unit for CIOs was 52 to 71%; for mail occurrences, 42 to 91%. All five CIOs served as a vital communications link.

Use of Technology

Ives and Olson (1981, 57) noted that "categorization by activities, purpose of contact, or message units tells only part of the story. Through observation we learned some revealing aspects of the nature of the job and the environment of the information systems manager." One observation was that information systems managers "seem to be among the last to directly benefit from the technology they purvey" (Ives and Olson 1981, 57). Only two of the six had terminals in their office. None used electronic mail and one used voice mail.

As has been noted, CIOs were users of information technology. All had terminals, four of five used electronic mail, four of five used voice mail, one used an Executive Support System, and another was evaluating Executive Support Systems. The insurance CIO who had never had responsibility outside of an information technology area was the most conservative user, limiting usage to incoming electronic mail and short notes. He did not use a personal computer at all. On the other hand, the university and utility CIOs, who had come from other areas, were users of information technology.

13

Participation in Strategic Planning

FACTORS AFFECTING CIO PARTICIPATION

Three factors were perceived to affect the CIOs' participation in strategy planning:

1. The industry's present or anticipated competitiveness
2. Personal and political acceptance by senior management
3. Authority to approve or disapprove information technology expenditures

Industry Competitiveness

The insurance company had changed its strategy, casting information technology into a critical role and anticipating increasingly intense competitive pressures. The utility company, anticipating deregulation, was restructuring to deploy its sizable information resources more efficiently and effectively. Pressures of the environment made the need for change in both organizations evident. The manufacturing company had anticipated a consolidation of the lighting manufacturers and used information technology to gain market share. The government agency sought a means to differentiate itself from other liberal arts schools as it competed for a dwindling pool of funds. Not surprisingly, in the organizations observed, environmental pressures either forced or encouraged the change represented by the use of information technology for a competitive advantage.

Acceptance

The personal and political acceptance of the utility, manufacturing, and government agency CIOs was evident. They were established powers within their organizations, with over 20 years' experience with their organizations. Two of the three had worked in other functional areas and one, whose career path had been in information systems, now had responsibility for product divisions as well. The utility CIO was a member of the Management Council; the manufacturing CIO was one of the Senior Seven; and the government agency CIO was a member of the site's Management Council.

IT Expenditure Authority

The resource allocator role was the critical role for CIOs. The extent to which it was played may be more dependent on organizational bureaucracy (authorization forms and levels of approval) than participation in strategic planning. However, the authority to approve information resources makes it advantageous for others in the organization to involve the CIO in strategic planning; and this involvement, in turn, gave the CIO criteria for resource allocation. One of the major benefits of restructuring for the utility company was to gain resource allocation authority for operating companies as well. This authority could then be leveraged to link policy, strategy, and information technology implementation.

MINTZBERG'S FRAMEWORK: OTHER DETERMINANTS

Mintzberg's framework for variables affecting a manager's work suggests other determinants for participation in strategic planning: job level and function, size of the organization, situational factors, and personality and style. Job level and function were made similar by the selection process. Other variables may be assessed on the basis of the observation experience rather than quantitative data.

Size

None of the companies could be described as small. The employees of the IT units numbered 108, 130, 120, 840 (1300 contract employees), and 700. The fact that the utility company IT unit had 700 employees did not seem to increase the CIO's participation in strategic planning compared to the manufacturing CIO, for example.

Situational Factors

The information intensity of the insurance company versus that of the manufacturing or utility company did not seem to give the insurance company CIO more importance in strategic planning. The high-tech milieu of the government agency CIO did not seem to give him an edge in strategic planning, either.

Personality and Style

Personality was a factor in the two situations in which the CIO was relatively new (two and six years) to the organization. The other three CIOs had been with their organizations for approximately 20 years, and the person and organization seemed well adjusted to each other.

In the first of the two situations in which the CIOs were relatively new, the university CIO was cognizant of the differences in his personality and the personality of university administration. In fact, he explained these differences to the observer. He described his background as that of a working-class Yankee operating in an aristocratic, Southern "good old boy" network. He felt that these differences were negatives which he must work to overcome. He had selected an administrative assistant who understood the university's protocol, and he sought her advice. When she felt he had handled a situation too abrasively and without the correct protocol, she said so privately. He created an office environment like that of many offices at the university. The CIO was a skilled tennis player and displayed his trophies. He was an avid reader and filled his office with a wide range of books, impressionist prints, and other mementos. His dress and his work habits were those of an academic. He did not seek to change his personality, but he did seek to adapt his manners to that of the environment, announcing in subtle ways that he could operate in this environment.

He commented to the observer, "It doesn't pay to make enemies at any level, even the janitor." He credited his upbringing in a multicultural environment to his awareness of differences and willingness to adapt to these differences. This CIO gave the nod, so the speak, to the milieu; but he asserted that he was hired because the university needed his aggressiveness and his ability to resist personal pressure when allocating resources. At the same time, he was in a precarious political position, lacking the support of an established insider. Personality and style could have created resistance and caused the President and Vice Provost to withdraw support.

In the insurance company, the CIO seemed to be a lamb following a lion because the former insurance company CIO had been very aggressive and powerful. Although the current CIO read *CIO* magazine, he introduced the observer as someone studying "the DP guy." In an industry becoming increasingly competitive and facing regulation of profits, information technology had assumed a powerful new position. He seemed to sense that trust, openness, and humility were needed in the aftermath of major change and to modulate his personality accordingly, keeping the door open with senior management, most of whom had been associated with the company since its founding. If he had not been so easy to deal with and nonthreatening, he might have been involved in strategic planning second hand, through the First Senior Vice President to whom he reported.

WORK CHARACTERISTICS ASSOCIATED WITH STRATEGIC PLANNING

Studying the characteristics of the strategic planning process for these CIOs has important implications, primary among which is to identify characteristics which may increase the participation for CIOs who sense that their participation is not what it should be. Prior studies have shown that most information executives are unsatisfied with their participation in strategic planning.

Six work characteristics for the strategic planning were analyzed (Stephens et al. 1994):

1. Location
2. Communication medium
3. Meeting size
4. Area of participants
5. Position of participants
6. Duration of activities.

Unlike the MIS manager who operates primarily within his or her own work area or is territory bound, the strategic responsibilities of the information executive should demand a broader territory. Therefore, the CIO's day-to-day responsibilities must not demand that he or she be on location in the information technology unit. Furthermore, the semistructured nature of strategic planning will force the need for richer communication mediums or face-to-face communications. The CIO's interaction pattern should show a high degree of interaction with other executives as he or she participates in strategic planning.

Because strategic planning should involve participants from many different functional areas, this face-to-face communication will employ scheduled meetings and activities of longer durations. Thus, communication with the CIO must not be necessary for the smooth day-to-day operation of the information technology unit.

Eight responsibilities were identified and used as coding classifications. The key responsibility was planning. Activities associated with all other responsibilities and with strategic planning were analyzed statistically, using hypotheses pertaining to each of the six work characteristics.

Location

Our first hypothesis pertained to location: Strategic planning will occur when the CIO is outside his or her territory (i.e., away from his or her office or a subordinate's office). Testing the difference of the average durations, this hypothesis is supported (a t test testing the null hypothesis that the average duration of strategic planning activities inside the CIO's territory is equal or greater than that outside the CIO's territory is rejected with a p value of .00095).

Because of the possibility of the occurrence of a few activities with extremely long durations, which could skew the distribution of activity times and therefore have a dominant effect on the mean, a nonparametric test for comparing locations of the two distributions was also conducted. The location hypothesis, that the strategic planning process will require that the CIO not be territory bound, was again supported. The Wilcoxon rank sum test was used to determine locational differences between the two distributions (activity durations inside the CIO's territory and those outside of it). The median duration was 14 minutes when the location was inside the CIO's territory and 40 minutes when the location was outside the CIO's territory. Again, a significant difference was found (p value of .00095). A work characteristic of strategic planning is that the CIO must be able to operate with ease outside the IT territory.

Communication Medium

Our second hypothesis pertained to communication medium. We hypothesized that the strategic planning process would require the use of richer mediums (i.e., face-to-face meetings versus phone calls or desk work). The data support the hypothesis that face-to-face interaction is a characteristic of these CIOs' participation in the strategic planning process (p value of .0003). Face-to-face communication skills are thus vital to the effective participation in strategic planning.

Number of Participants

Our third hypothesis pertained to the number of participants in strategic planning activities. The hypothesis that strategic planning activities will require a larger number of participants in meetings than would meetings pertaining to other responsibilities was confirmed. That is, the meeting size of strategic planning activities was found to be significantly different from meetings focused on other CIO responsibilities (a test for determining whether the average number of participants in strategic planning activities exceeds that for other activities was conducted, yielding a (*p* value of .00325).

The strategic planning process requires participation in larger meetings. However, a similar set of hypotheses was tested when the medium is only scheduled meetings. The data were probed further by hypothesizing that scheduled meetings, whose purpose was strategic planning, would involve more participants than other scheduled meetings. Our prior hypothesis involved all meetings, both scheduled and unscheduled. However, this hypothesis was not supported (p value of .0771 for a level of significance of .05). Surprisingly, informal gatherings or unscheduled meetings were larger if the activity focus was strategic planning, but formal scheduled meetings were not. This finding provides quantitative support for the perception that personal and political acceptance or informal acceptance is critical to participation in strategic planning. Large, informal, unscheduled meetings were important for participation.

Interaction Patterns

Our fourth hypothesis related to building those informal relationships for strategic planning. We hypothesized that strategic planning activities require the CIO to interact more with those outside the information technology area, from the environment and functional areas, than with those within the IT group.

Two groups of participants were formed, one including those from the information technology unit and one including those from other functional areas and the environment. The hypothesis was supported when a test involving the number of participants in strategic planning activities was performed (*p* value of .00975). The data were probed further, with tests of the duration of strategic planning activities involving those within the IT group versus those outside the group. Despite the increased average duration time for activities outside the information technology area over those within, the difference was not statistically significant (p value of .3599). The CIO participating in strategic planning need not spend more time with those outside the IT group, but the time spent outside the group will involve more people.

Participant Positions

The fifth of the six work characteristics hypotheses pertained to the position of those participating in strategic planning. We hypothesized that for strategic planning, the CIO must interact with a greater number of peers and superiors than he or she does for other responsibilities. When the communication medium is desk work or mail, no significant difference was found (*p* value of .4245) in the number of peers involved with strategic planning versus other responsibilities. This finding was also the case when the medium was unscheduled meeting (*p* value of .3983). However, when the medium was scheduled meeting, the mean number of peers for strategic planning activities exceeds that for activities (*t* of 2.536, *p* value of .0063). So, while the number of participants in scheduled meetings are not different for strategic planning, the position of participants does differ, as would be expected.

A similar analysis was conducted for the number of superiors with whom a CIO interacts. In investigating whether the average number of superiors for strategic planning activities exceeds that for other activities, no significant differences were found when the medium is scheduled meeting (*p* value of .1287) or unscheduled meeting (*p* value of .0893). Interestingly, however, when the medium is desk work or mail, the average number of superiors for strategic planning activities exceeds that for other activities (*p* value of .0320).

A follow-up analysis was conducted to investigate further this finding. One objective was to determine if the proportion of activities, rather than the average number of superiors, in which a superior is present is greater for strategic planning activities. The data supported the conclusion that the proportion of activities in which a superior is present is greater for strategic planning activities than for other activities (a test conducted for the difference of proportions yielded a test statistic of Z of 3.3 with a *p* value < .001). Surprisingly, no significant difference was found in this proportion when the medium was scheduled meeting. However, when the medium is desk work or mail, the proportion of strategic planning activities in which a superior is present is greater than that for other activities (Z of 3.319, *p* value < .001). A similar conclusion was drawn when the medium was the informal or unscheduled meeting ($Z=2.298$, *p* value$=0.0107$). The written medium and informal meetings were important vehicles for strategic planning involving the CIO with his or her superior.

Since the medium of desk work or mail demonstrated the highest proportion of interaction of superiors for strategic planning, an analysis of incoming and outgoing desk work or mail was conducted. For strategic planning, interaction with a superior mainly takes place through incoming mail (62.50% of the time) as opposed to outgoing mail (37.50% of the time). A similar pattern is observed for other activities: the CIO is receiving mail more frequently from a superior than he or she is sending it. The CEO or position superior to the CIO was initiating an exchange with the CIO.

Further analysis was conducted to see if this direction of mail flow was dependant on the strategic planning responsibility (a chi-square test was conducted yielding a test statistic of 4.780 with a p value of 0.029 for .05 level of significance). Activities focusing on the responsibility of strategic planning involving the CIO's superior were associated with more incoming than outgoing mail, compared with activities regarding other responsibilities. These CIOs' superiors were actively engaged in making the CIO an informed member of the strategic planning team and the written medium was used to do so. By implication, these CEOs found the CIOs involvement important to the organization. This quantitative evidence relates to the observer's perception that an intensely competitive environment facilitated the CIO's involvement in strategic planning. Further, the superior's use of the informal or unscheduled meeting indicates a comfort level with the CIO, and to a degree, personal and political acceptance.

One CIO used the written medium to cement his participation. At the manufacturing company, where the CEO and CIO had received the SIM Partners in Excellence Award, the CIO had volunteered to "write up" every strategic planning meeting. He jokingly called himself the company scribe. He then distributed his summary of the meetings to all participants and always sent a copy to the CEO or any absent peer. He commented that putting the meeting in written form gave him a subtle power to shape strategy, since his interpretation became the record. He also became an essential member of any strategic planning meeting and was strongly associated with the process.

Duration of Strategic Planning Activities

Our final hypothesis sought to verify the time requirements of strategic planning. We hypothesized that strategic planning will require uninterrupted activities of longer duration. With the methodology used for this study, an interruption would constitute a change in activity and thus cause a shorter activity duration. An important implication of this duration hypothesis and of the location hypothesis is that the CIO must not be an integral part of the information technology unit's day-to-day functioning if he or she is to be able to participate in strategic planning. This process would require absences from the unit and absences of longer duration. The data strongly support this hypothesis (a statistical test conducted to determine whether the average duration of strategic planning activities exceeded that of other activities yielded a test statistic of t of 4.1068, with a p value $< .00005$).

Implications of Work Characteristics

Implications of this study of five successful CIOs, all of whom participate in organizational strategic planning to varying degrees, are as follows:

- The CIO must operate outside the information technology territory, facilitating informal exchanges or unscheduled meetings, and interact with those from other functional areas. Geography is important. Two CIOs found that locating their office outside the information technology unit had been beneficial.

- The CIO must be skilled in face-to-face communication. Most of the process occurs during large, long-lasting scheduled meetings with participants from outside the information technology unit. These participants do not use the language of the information technology unit.

- The written medium is an important channel to the CIO's superior and a way to improve participation in the process.

Finally and foremost, the characteristics of the strategic planning process are such that a CIO who is essential to the smooth, day-to-day functioning of the information technology unit cannot be a participant. The dilemma is how to stay up to date with the technology, a key expectation of peers and superiors, and not be intimately involved in the day-to-day functioning.

14

Conclusions

BASIS OF CONCLUSIONS

Conclusions are based on the observation of five successful CIOs in five industry types for 215 hours, involving 501 verbal contacts and 464 pieces of mail. Conclusions are also based on my discussions with CIOs during meals, travel time, walks to conference rooms, and after working hours.

Of the nine elements coded, five were straightforward and required few inferences:

1. Communication medium employed (phone call, scheduled meeting, unscheduled meeting, tour, and desk work or written mediums)
2. Place (10 coded locations)
3. Area of each participant (external, other functional units, information technology unit)
4. Participant title (10 coded titles)
5. Initiate (self, other, mutual, or regularly scheduled)

The other four elements were inferential to varying degrees. These elements, as well as anecdotal data, served as a valuable guide, however:

1. Attention level (skim, read, study)
2. Purpose (69 categories and subcategories)
3. Role (Mintzberg's ten managerial roles)
4. Responsibility (common responsibilities areas from literature review)

In each case, the observation week was thought to representative. Comparisons of the profile for these CIOs with the CIOs participating in Brumm's (1988b) study of *Fortune* 100 CIOs showed the profiles to be similar. However, general conclusions cannot be made without due caution. CIOs observed were carefully selected from varying industry groups because they had a record of achievement and success as a CIO.

THE CIO'S STRUCTURE AND VALUE GOAL

Synnott and Gruber (1981), who first employed the term *CIO*, cites a twofold objective for this new managerial role: a value goal, or providing a competitive advantage for the firm, and a structure goal, or participating in restructuring the firm and the technology unit. This restructuring is to improve flexibility or improve the organization's ability to adapt to change.

Structure Goal

In the diverse organizations observed, the value goal and structure goal were highly interrelated, with restructuring being a means to the value goal of competitive advantage. As has been discussed, each organization had undergone a restructuring in the last two years.

Simplification

The utility company sought to restructure information resource units as a preliminary step to restructuring the entire organization. Although organizations which had restructured were flatter, the restructuring seemed geared toward what Keen (1987) called a simplification rather than Drucker's (1988) decentralization.

Common areas had been sought and areas combined. In the insurance company, decentralized project teams had been replaced by process groups: analysis, design, implementation, operations, and technical services. In the university, academic and administrative computing groups had been combined into one division. In the manufacturing company, support for systems within the company and in the field had been combined. In the government agency, two divisions (telecommunications and information systems) had been combined and the agency was seeking further ways to combine both information resource units and engineering project teams. As Keen (1987) indicated, the complexity of the organizations had led to a need for simplification.

The CIO as Network Manager

Network architecture was a priority issue with the manufacturing company, government agency, and utility company. Neither the insurance company nor the university was communicating on a regular basis with geographically dispersed sites. The insurance company did receive transmissions from Japan periodically and is now communicating regularly with dispersed sales agents. The network at the government agency was by far the most complex, providing critical access to sites all over the world and to academic and research institutions using a wide array of software and hardware. More than any other CIO, the government agency CIO could be called a network manager. Other CIOs were working toward a client-server model which would give customization and query capability to users, eliminating what the insurance CIO called "significant demand."

The CIO as Change Agent

Intensifying competitive forces led companies observed to use information technology as a competitive weapon and to include the CIO as an integral member of the top management strategic planning team. Information technology had provided competitive advantage, requiring and/or accompanied by a restructuring of the information technology unit and other organizational units. The effort was more to simplify on the basis of common functions than to decentralize. Each CIO was an active change agent within his group and within the organization, confirming M. Scott Morton's assertion (Kolodziej, 1989) and LaRosa's (1985) dissertation conclusions: CIOs must be general managers and managers of change.

Value Goal

In each organization, as would be expected in an organization hosting a successful CIO, information technology was used for competitive advantage. The manufacturing company had used electronic links with sales agents early on to prosper and gain market share in the lighting industry, while other companies fell by the wayside and the industry consolidated. This company still aggressively pursues the advantage gained and is differentiating the product offered to contractors by bundling critical information about product delivery with the product. The lighting company has created barriers to entry and raised the switching costs of its sales agents, contractors, and distributors. For 20 years, the CIO has been the champion of investing in systems which enhance market share rather than systems which merely automate clerical labor.

The utility company is working to lower the threat of new entrants into its market when the industry is deregulated. Common systems and a new information resources structure, as well as new organization structure, should provide an economy of scale which cannot be matched by smaller, new entrants. In a deregulated environment, this utility company can provide cost leadership. The

CIO has led the way for restructuring by going first, often placing himself in precarious positions with operating company presidents as his own job was restructured.

The insurance company is using information technology to enter new supplemental insurance markets, with few additional resources.   It is also differentiating its insurance products by the quality of information services bundled with the product: rapid claims processing times and quick turnarounds on requests for information or status reports. The CIO, who has worked at the revenue-producing Japan branch for the past two years, has served as a catalyst. He is careful to maintain client involvement in this change averse organization, making sure that clients champion technology implementation. His priority has been establishing trust, what Stephen Covey has called the key to "the new management mindset" which makes people more productive (McNurith 1988b, 14).

The government agency, faced with funding cuts and competing allotments to other agencies, is improving its cost and quality performance with improved information resource management. The CIO is taking a process engineering and Total Quality Management approach to streamline and simplify processes and systems.

At the university, the liberal arts education provided is differentiated by being computer intense for students, faculty, and the administration. This CIO was hired because of his well-publicized views on the importance of a computer intense creating academic environment. In fact, he was hired to make it happen.

A PARADIGM SHIFT

Quantitative analysis of the CIOs and MIS managers observed indicated that the CIO, like the CEO and unlike the MIS manager, was functioning as a general manager rather than a functional manager or staff specialist.   The boundaries and what must be done to be successful within those boundaries have changed.

What Barker (1985) described as a paradigm shift has occurred. According to Covey (McNurith 1988b, 14)," to make significant changes, people need to change how they solve problems and how they view the world—they need to make a paradigm shift." A role change has occurred for the information manager. And according to Covey (McNurith 1988b, 14), "one way to cause a paradigm shift is to change someone's role."

Interaction patterns for all five CIOs observed showed them spending more than half their verbal contact time outside the information technology group. All CIOs were not only official members of senior management but also seemed to have informal acceptance in four of the five observations.

Characteristics of the Successful CIO

O'Riordan's (1987) six characteristics of the successful CIO proved an apt description for the five CIOs observed for a total of 215 work hours:

- Be a business person.
- Be able to maintain an overall view of business needs.
- Be able to cross department boundaries.
- Understand technology from a business perspective.
- Be innovative and flexible.
- Be able to communicate well.

Three of the CIOs were long-term veterans of their companies. The other two had worked in the same industry for 15 years before their present position. The manufacturing CIO asserted to every applicant interviewed that he or she must be a businessperson first. Experience in other functional areas as well as long-term employment in the organization gave these CIOs the ability to maintain an overall view of business needs and seemed to facilitate boundary spanning. Three of the five CIOs had worked in other functional areas before assuming responsibility in an information technology unit. Not only did they know these areas' functions, but they had also developed informal relationships.

CIOs observed communicated well in verbal and written mediums. Delivering presentations or speeches was an important task. During the five observation weeks, two senior management presentations were delivered (utility, manufacturing), two presentations for information technology groups were delivered (insurance company meeting, university service awards), and the university CIO spent time preparing a presentation for the National Science Foundation. All five used analogies as a powerful communication tool. Written communication was also critical because this was a primary medium for important strategy and policy plans.

CIO Responsibilities

The literature review identified eight common responsibilities for CIOs and these responsibilities were made a coding element. If these common responsibilities are grouped into short-term and long-term responsibilities, the long-term responsibilities account for three fourths of all mail and verbal contacts. These results agree with those of LaRosa (1985, 37). During one of her 11 interviews, a CIO commented, "You're thinking out further ahead, trying to establish directions and trends." Of the common responsibilities from the literature review, education as the primary purpose for an activity seemed insignificant. However, education was often a part of an activity which primarily involved strategic planning with other senior managers.

Table 14.1
CIO Responsibilities

Long-term Responsibilities	Percent of mail and verbal contacts
Policies, procedures	6%
Strategic planning	12%
Expenditures	22%
Coordination	24%
Environmental scanning	11%
Education	1%
Short term responsibilities	
Consulting, present problems	6%
Other general managerial	18%

The strategic planning responsibility was most time consuming (35% of the time, although it constituted only 16% of occurrences). Coordination of the IT group, other functional units, and the environment, or acting as a bridge, ranked second (21% of time). Over half of the CIOs verbal contact time was devoted to these two responsibilities. Empirical evidence does suggest, then, that the CIO as a bridge—linking business strategy and information technology, linking information technology units to other units and the environment—is an accurate picture.

These results are similar to the roles analysis, with the difference that the resource allocator role has a much broader meaning than the approval or acceptance of expenditures for information technology. Resource allocator also includes allocation of the manager's own time or scheduling and human resource decisions.

Maintaining Equilibrium

Sayles (1964, 256) used unstructured observation to study managerial work (i.e, he observed without coding activities for subsequent quantitative analysis). His description seems especially appropriate for CIOs observed. He describes managerial work as an open system in which "a variety of administrative patterns" are adopted "to fit the varying requirements of the interface: where his job meets others." In the manager's effort to maintain a "moving equilibrium," the manager may change his or her behavior or that of others or change the organizational structure.

Paradoxically, the changes observed were an attempt to remain the same, an "equilibrium." The utility company wished to remain the dominant force in the new deregulated environment. The insurance company wished to continue to grow at predictable rates of return. The lighting company wished to continue as the leader of the lighting industry. The university sought to maintain its reputation for providing a first-rate education by providing students and faculty with the tools of information technology. The government agency sought to provide the quality product, in terms of services and science/engineering projects, for which it had become famous.

Participating in Planning

Management Roles

Mintzberg's framework for managerial roles suggests that rank is a necessary but not sufficient condition for the CIO's involvement in strategic decisions. Given the appropriate rank or formal authority and status, interpersonal roles, particularly the liaison role, must place the CIO in the position to play informational roles. Being privy to information prepares the CIO to participate in strategy formulation. The CIO must then gain the personal and political acceptance of senior management, or must also acquire informal authority, if he or she is to participate as a partner in strategic planning.

Information, both formal and informal, made the CIO capable of participating in strategic planning in a meaningful way. However, the CIO was both a source and recipient of information. The decisional roles of resource allocator and entrepreneur were, at the same time, dependent on his participation in strategy/policy sessions and a primary reason for his participation. The decisional roles were both cause and effect. The authority of the resource allocator role acted as a lever for informal acceptance and opened channels of information. This role, used effectively, further enhanced the CIO's status within the organization and was an essential part of the formal and informal authority granted him. The resource allocator role was the single most important managerial role.

Perceived Determinants of Participation

The study selection criterion assumed the formal authority and status of a

CIO. Three determinants of participation in strategic planning were discerned: present or anticipated competitiveness in the industry's environment, personal and political acceptance by senior management, and the authority to approve or disapprove expenditures for information technology. Given formal authority along with or even because of intensifying competitive forces, the CIO needs informal acceptance or personal and political acceptance among senior managers. The CIO's role as resource allocator, approving or disapproving information technology expenditures, facilitates this acceptance but may be dependent upon this acceptance. While strategic planning tended to be a group verbal contact activity, CIOs prepared for participation in solitary desk work sessions.

Work Characteristics

An analysis of these five CIOs' work characteristics, all of whom participated in strategic planning, reveals clearly that CIOs who are on the strategy team must operate outside the IT territory, both in terms of location and those with whom they interact. Surprisingly, the written medium was an important communication channel with the CIOs' superiors, and the superior tended to initiate the exchange. Informal meetings were especially important for interaction with peers and superiors. Communication skills, both oral and written, are necessary. Participation in strategic planning requires the ability to hold one's own in large, long meetings. Four of the CIOs observed were forceful public speakers (one was not observed delivering a presentation).

Successful CIO Facts

Mintzberg (1975) framed his conclusions concerning managerial work in four folklore and fact sets. The CIOs' work may be described by modifying Mintzberg's description. First, the five successful CIOs observed are reflective people, considering situations, people, environmental pressures with sensitivity and care. This reflection or introspection is sometimes in process, or an ongoing part of verbal interactions, and sometimes isolated, occurring at the CIO's desk or at home, aided by the written medium.   Each CIO seemed highly interested in his work as well as the work of other CIOs. All were interested in the study and seemed eager to discuss questions relating to their work whenever the opportunity arose (travel time, for the most part, or during meals).

Some CIOs work at paces requiring high stamina but seem to relish this pace. Others carefully control their pace and their time. Activities, as measured by change in participants and/or medium, are characterized by brevity and variety but also by continuity. The CIOs' current agendas act as a center of gravity, turning all events toward them and providing coherence for activities. These

CIOs have a bias for action but are not averse to reflective activities. In fact, they create a special time for such activities in their schedules.

Second, the regular duties which these CIOs perform are largely of their own choosing. Handling exceptions or disturbance handling is an important role, but regular duties (such as resource allocation, entrepreneurial activities, and monitoring) are as, if not more, important. Each CIO, to a greater or lesser degree, had taken an active role in creating his present position and continued to shape the role within the organization.

Third, CIOs use the richer, often more efficient, verbal contact mediums about twice as much as the written medium but find the written medium particularly important for strategy and policy summaries and for environmental scanning. Some standard aggregated information or reports are routinely reviewed as guideposts to performance. One CIO used an Executive Support System. Customized or special request reports are just as common as those standard or common reports.

Three CIOs commented that electronic mail provides access not available through verbal mediums while, like the verbal contact mediums, being current. Four of the CIOs observed used e-mail to communicate directly with those many layers under them on a hierarchy chart. To some degree, the written medium of e-mail worked to prevent the executive's disease, isolation. So, unlike Mintzberg's finding, the written medium was a valued one.

Fourth, the CIOs' work is multidimensional and complex, a "moving equilibrium." Organizations are complex, open systems. To describe the management of these systems as a science or a profession in terms of specialized knowledge may presume an oversimplified view of the system. How the CIOs accomplished the multifaceted tasks assigned to them bore a greater resemblance to the work of a playwright than to that of a scientist. Rather than being able to discern cause and effect using the scientific method, the tasks involved a high level of nuance and ambiguity. Staging and timing events, selecting characters to involve, and choosing words with certain connotations were considered crucial decisions. Certainly, as has been observed in CIO interviews, surveys, and the prescriptive literature, communication skills were critical.

CIO AS BRIDGE

The CIO is functioning as an executive (i.e., strategically) and the characteristics of the work and managerial roles resemble that found in Mintzberg's study and others. The information executive's job, the CIO'S job, is different from that of the staff specialist or functional manager, the MIS manager, or the DP manager, as manifested by differences in work characteristics and interaction patterns. The interaction pattern (or distribution of activities among the information technology group, functional groups, and external groups) along with specific responsibilities, largely confirms the prescriptive literature which portrays the CIO as the bridge between the three groups.

How the difficult job of bridging the gap between business units and information technology groups and linking both to the environment was accomplished may have been best described by Sayles (1964, 256), "moving equilibrium." The CIOs observed were skilled readers of situations and other people, generally demonstrating high levels of empathy. They did not play the role of technical experts, although each had extensive experience with information technology. They often pretended ignorance and were self-effacing to encourage others to speak freely. They recognized the need to fit in to their organizations and conformed to customary dress and conduct.

These CIOs chose their timing and their words carefully and took what one CIO called "word smithing" very seriously. Looking at situations from others' points of view is related to the careful choice of words and use of analogies. This ability to assume other points of view went beyond empathy. All CIOs observed demonstrated a remarkable detachment in the face of emotional conflicts and/or highly frustrating situations.

After over 200 hours spent observing five CIOs in some extraordinarily difficult, even sloppy, situations, the abiding image is that of holding another's point of view aloft, as if it were a multifaceted crystal object, passing light through it, seeking its strengths and weaknesses, and remaining detached but not uninvolved, delicately balancing reflection and action. This ability is an art and a science.

Mintzberg (1975, 59) noted that "no job is more vital to our society than that of a manager." At this juncture in the Information Age, perhaps no manager is more vital than the CIO—lest we become "the tools of our tools" (Thoreau 1854, 32).

Appendix A:

Observation Forms

Appendix A.1 **Checklist for Preliminary Data**	
General:	
1	Copy of appointment calendar for one month
2	CIO resume
3	Staff size
4	Areas of responsibility
5	Organizational chart for areas of responsibility
6	Organization chart
7	Identification of most frequent contacts
8	Telecommunications network chart
9	Any articles, books in which the CIO is mentioned
10	Manager's work habits
Organization:	
1	Locations of company (geographical dispersion)
2	Annual reports for three years
3	Organization's mission
4	Size of organization in terms of employees and assets
5	Relevant financial data
6	Industry characteristics

Appendix A.1, continued
Checklist for Preliminary Data

Observer's initial visit:

1	Observe for • indications of company culture • managerial style
2	Talk with CIO concerning protocol of observation • where to sit for observing • how to deal with questions/need for clarification • if copies may be made of some mail documents for clarification • manager's willingness to "talk through" his desk-work activities as he performs them so that the mail record can be completed

Appendix A.2
Variables Coded

1	Medium employed	Call (C), Scheduled Meeting (SM), Unscheduled Meeting (UM), Tour (T), Desk work (D). If the medium were desk work, Incoming and outgoing desk work, the form of mail (letter, memo, clipping, report, periodical), and attention level were coded.
2	Place	10 coded locations
3	Area of each participant	External to the firm or from the environment (E), from another functional area (F) such as marketing, from the Information Technology unit (IT)
4	Participant title	10 coded titles
5	Initiate	Self (X), other (initiate's participant title code), mutual (M), or regularly scheduled (C for clock)
6	Attention level	Skim (Sk), read (R), study (S)
7	Purpose	Mintzberg's 69 categories and subcategories
8	Role	Mintzberg's managerial roles framework
9	Responsibility	8 common responsibility areas from a review of the prescriptive literature, one of which is strategic planning

Appendix A.3 Coding Keys		
Code Title	Code Location	Code-Specific Responsibilities
1 Subordinate	1 Manager's office	1 Policies, procedures, general guideline setting
2 Director (superior)	2 Subordinate's office	2 Strategic planning (specific, prior to capital acquisition)
3 Peer internal	3 Superior's office	3 Approval, acceptance of expenditures
4 Peer external	4 Hall	4 Coordination of 3 groups: IT, F, E
5 Trade organization	5 Plant	5 Education
6 Client	6 Conference room	6 Consulting (present problems)
7 Supplier or vendor	7 Board room	7 Other general managerial
8 Independent	8 Away from organization	8 Environment scanning
9 Publisher	9 Home	
10 Government	10 Peer office	

Appendix A.3, continued
Coding Keys

Roles:

1 Figurehead	Ceremonial—greet touring dignitaries, customer to lunch, attend wedding
*2 Leader	Within-unit work
*3 Liaison	Contacts outside the vertical chain of command I and E
4 Monitor	Scans environment, questions contacts, subordinates, receives information from network of contacts
5 Disseminate	Information to/among subs who would not have otherwise
6 Spokesman	Speech, prod mod to supplier, speak for unit to supervisor
7 Entrepreneur	Voluntarily seeks to improve w/ projects, ideas
8 Disturbance Handler	Involuntarily responding to pressures too severe to ignore
9 Resource Allocator	Who gets what, allocates own time, unit's structure, authorizes the important decisions of unit
10 Negotiator	Work out contract, grievance settlement
*Not coded	

Appendix A.4
Mintzberg's Purpose Categories for Mail Coding Keys

Categories   Subcategories

	1 Acknowledgments		
Incoming Mail	2 Status requests	a	Peers for donation to charity
		b	Signature only
		c	Independent ?'s, donations to charity
	3 Solicitations sell product, provide service, participate in seminar		
	4 Authority requests	a	Exception to normal procedures
		b	Approval new program, procedures
		c	Acceptance of a policy, resource commitment, job applicants
	5 Reference data	a	Inside Organization meeting agendas, resumes for new employee
		b	External for org as much as for manager annual reports
		c	External scheduling such as trade shows
	6 General reports	a	Manager request
		b	Unrequested
	7 Periodical news	a	General
		b	Management
		c	Trade
		d	Business/financial
		e	Political
		f	Technological
		g	House organs
		h	Book
	8 Events in environment	a	Organization to environment clipping of an article about environment
		b	Upcoming trade organization events
		c	Notices of personal contacts, competitors, clients, trade events
		d	Political

Appendix A.4, continued
Mintzberg's Purpose Categories for Mail Coding Keys

Categories   Subcategories

```
                                      ┌ a  Regular internal
Incoming │9 Reports on operations ───┤ b  Ad hoc
Mail     │                            └ c  Unsolicited letters

         │ 10 Advice on situations (usually strategic)
         │ 11 Problems and pressures clearly defined, why no donation (like
         │    manager's request)
         │ 12 Ideas
         └─────────────────────────
```

```
         ┌─────────────────────────
Outgoing │ 13 Acknowledge input
Mail     │ 14 Reply to written request
         │ 15 Reply to information received
         │ 16 Forward information to subordinate
         │ 17 Forward request to subordinate
         │ 18 Write to 3rd party re input
         │ 19 Acknowledge/reply to verbal contact
         │ 20 Write report
         │ 21 Originate letter/memo
         └─────────────────────────
```

Appendix A.4, continued
Mintzberg's Purpose Categories for Verbal Contacts

Verbal Contact

```
22 Nonmanagerial work
23 Scheduling brief informal for purpose of scheduling time
24 Ceremony greet new employee, plaque, speak to visiting group,
   attend funeral
25 External board work
26 Status requests/solicitations (speak at function, join board,
   send document)
```

27 Action requests
other request of manager

- a Authorization new program or policy or exception to existing
- b Information plans, policies, meeting missed
- c initiate would manager make a certain point at a meeting?
- d Influencing pressures exerted on manager job candidates, promotion

28 Manager requests
manager requests of others

- a Information/advice can you hire friend? know about ad?
- b Delegated task
- c Follow-ups on previous requests

29 Observational tours

30 Receiving information

- a Instant communication very current
- b Briefings presentations, analysis
- c Interviewing employees, attend conference, listen

31 Giving information

- a Instant communication
- b Plans and policies
- c Advice how to handle a sales negotiation

32 Review

- a Deputy close subordinate meetings to review what's happening
- b Functional
- c Contact usually personal to trade rumors, political advice
- d New man
- e Post meeting review a few stay over to discuss certain items
- f Organizational board meetings

Appendix A.4, continued
Mintzberg's Purpose Categories for Verbal Contacts

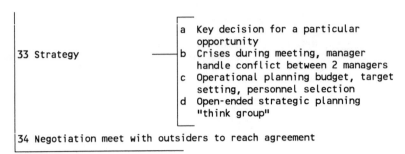

		a	Key decision for a particular opportunity
33 Strategy		b	Crises during meeting, manager handle conflict between 2 managers
		c	Operational planning budget, target setting, personnel selection
		d	Open-ended strategic planning "think group"

34 Negotiation meet with outsiders to reach agreement

Appendix B:

Mintzberg's Analysis Replicated

Appendix B.1
Analysis of Chronology Record

Category	Study Composite	Ins.	Univ.	Manf.	Govt.	Util.
		MRG A	MRG B	MRG C	MRG D	MRG E
*Total hours work	214.9	39.25	49.62	46.47	35.47	44.12
**Hours in travel (not included)	7.24	3.02	2.08	1.88	.25	0
Hours of evening meetings	4.50	0	0	4.50	0	0
Total amount of mail	464.	60	106	47	129	122
Avg mail processed/day	19	12	21	9	26	24
Total number of activities	623	148	118	94	137	126
Desk Work:						
No. of sessions	122	19	36	12	20	35
Time on desk work (hours)	59.45	5.42	25.28	8.70	5.25	14.8
Average duration (mins)	29	17	42	44	16	25
Proportion of time	28%	14%	51%	19%	15%	34%
Telephone Calls:						
Number of calls	174	21	32	30	51	40
Time on telephone (hours)	18.63	1.18	3.25	5.80	5.28	3
Average duration (mins)	6	3	6	12	6	5
Proportion of time	9%	3%	7%	12%	15%	7%

Category	Study Composite	Ins.	Univ.	Manf	Govt	Util.
		MGR A	MGR B	MGR C	MRG D	MRG E
Appendix B.1, continued **Analysis of Chronology Record**						
Scheduled Meetings:						
Number of meetings	109	16	18	30	27	18
Time in meetings (hours)	103.2	19.42	16.52	26	19.73	21.48
Average duration (minutes)	59	73	55	52	44	72
Proportion of time	48%	49%	33%	56%	56%	49%
Unscheduled Meetings:						
No. of meetings	176	66	30	20	37	23
Time in meetings (hours)	30.33	10.83	4.25	6	5.13	4.32
Average duration (minutes)	11	10	8.5	17.4	8	11
Proportion of time	14%	28%	9%	12%	14%	10%
Tours:						
Number of tours	42	26	2	2	2	10
Time in tours (hours)	3.36	2.4	.32	.17	.07	.4
Average duration (minutes)	6	6	9.5	5	2	2.4
Proportion of time	2%	6%	1%	0%	0%	1%
Proportion of activities lasting 9 min 60 min	54% 9%	61% 6%	46% 9%	41% 19%	58% 4%	58% 10%

* MGR D took five hours vacation Friday afternoon
** Travel included in total hours worked when work conducted during travel,
   as was usually the case.

Appendix B.2
Analysis of Contact Record

Category	Study Com-posite	Ins.	Univ.	Manuf.	Govt. Agency	Util.
		MRG A	MRG B	MRG C	MRG D	MRG E
Total verbal contacts (hrs)	155	33.83	24.33	37.77	30.22	29.32
Total number of verbal contacts	501	129	82	82	177	91
Media: Percent of Contacts/Percent of Contact Time						
Telephone calls	35% / 12%	16% / 3%	39% / 13%	37% / 15%	44% / 17%	44% / 11%
Scheduled meetings (SM)	22% / 66%	12% / 57%	22% / 68%	37% / 69%	23% / 65%	20% / 73%
Unscheduled meetings (UM)	35% / 20%	51% / 32%	37% / 17%	24% / 15%	32% / 17%	25% / 15%
Tours	8% / 2%	20% / 7%	2% / 1%	2% / 0%	2% / 0%	11% / 1%
* Participants: Percent of Contacts/Percent of Contact Time						
Subordinate	64% / 49%	77% / 43%	58% / 48%	51% / 39%	58% / 59%	71% / 62%
Director (Superior)	5% / 8%	3% / 13%	9% / 6%	6% / 9%	7% / 6%	3% / 4%
Co-director (Peer internal)	11% / 16%	12% / 31%	8% / 12%	9% / 9%	16% / 17%	10% / 9%
Peer external and trade organization	4% / 6%	0% / 0%	1% / 0%	18% / 23%	0% / 0%	3% / 1%
Client	3% / 3%	0% / 0%	15% / 13%	2% / 4%	1% / 0%	0% / 0%
Supplier or vendor	8% / 11%	7% / 13%	4% / 11%	3% / 4%	14% / 18%	10% / 12%

Appendix B.2, continued Analysis of Contact Record						
Category	Study Com-posite	Ins.	Univ.	Manuf.	Govt. Agency	Util.
		MRG A	MRG B	MRG C	MRG D	MRG E
Independent and other	4% 7%	1% 0%	4% 9%	11% 13%	4% 0%	2% 3%
Form of Initiation: Percent of Total Contacts						
Manager	49%	84% 65%	33% 40%	28% 34%	57% 49%	41% 45%
Opposite party	40%	31% 24%	35% 43%	43% 52%	46% 39%	45% 49%
Mutual	9%	14% 11%	11% 13%	7% 9%	10% 9%	4% 4%
Clock	2%	0% 0%	3% 4%	4% 5%	4% 3%	1% 1%

Appendix B.2, continued
Analysis of Contact Record

Category	Study Composite	Ins.	Univ.	Manf.	Govt. Agency	Util.
		MGR A	MGR B	MGR C	MGR D	MGR E
Location: Percent of Contacts/Percent of Time						
Manager's office	53% 33%	40% 18%	65% 56%	12% 8%	79% 60%	65% 39%
Office of subordinate	7% 5%	12% 4%	6% 4%	5% 1%	6% 8%	5% 9%
Office of superior	1% 1%	2% 1%	4% 1%	0% 0%	1% 1%	0% 0%
Hall or plant	16% 7%	35% 15%	16% 10%	4% 1%	6% 7%	14% 2%
Conference or board room	10% 26%	2% 22%	6% 17%	33% 46%	8% 15%	4% 25%
Away from organization	12% 27%	8% 39%	2% 10%	46% 44%	1% 9%	11% 25%
Peer's office	1% 1%	2% 1%	1% 2%	0% 0%	0% 0%	0% 0%
Purpose of contact: Percent of Contacts/Percent of Contact Time						
Non managerial*	.2% 1%	0% 0%	0% 0%	0% 0%	1% 3%	0% 0%
Scheduling	13% 5%	11% 2%	12% 12%	21% 6%	12% 4%	12% 3%
Ceremony	5% 5%	2% 6%	5% 8%	4% 1%	2% 3%	13% 8%
External Board Work	.4% 2%	0% 0%	0% 0%	2% 7%	0% 0%	0% 0%
Total Secondary	19% 12%	13% 8%	17% 20%	27% 14%	14% 10%	25% 11%

Category	Study Composite	Ins.	Univ.	Manf.	Govt. Agency	Util.
		MGR A	MGR B	MGR C	MGR D	MGR E
Status requests and solicitations	3% 1%	2% 1%	1% 0%	2% 2%	2% 2%	8% 1%
Action requests	10% 4%	9% 4%	13% 9%	6% 4%	15% 4%	7% 1%
Manager requests	13% 3%	12% 5%	13% 5%	1% 0%	18% 5%	16% 3%
Total Requests/ Solicitations	26% 9%	23% 10%	28% 14%	10% 6%	34% 11%	31% 5%
Observational Tours	2% 1%	9% 2%	0% 0%	0% 0%	0% 0%	0% 0%
Receiving information	9% 13%	16% 23%	12% 10%	7% 5%	3% 13%	3% 16%
Giving information	11% 8%	17% 10%	9% 4%	10% 13%	15% 10%	3% 1%
Review	19% 24%	19% 21%	22% 28%	30% 37%	14% 16%	14% 14%
Total Information	0% 45%	60% 56%	43% 42%	48% 55%	32% 39%	21% 31%
Strategy	13% 31%	3% 25%	11% 18%	16% 25%	16% 31%	23% 53%
Negotiation	1% 3%	0% 0%	1% 6%	0% 0%	3% 8%	0% 0%
Total Decision Making	14% 33%	3% 25%	12% 24%	16% 25%	20% 40%	23% 53%

Appendix B.2, continued
Analysis of Contact Record

Appendix B.2, continued
Analysis of Contact Record

Size of SM (Scheduled Meetings) UM (Unscheduled Meetings) Tours	Com- posite SM UM T	MGR A SM UM T	MGR B SM UM T	MGR C SM UM T	MGR D SM UM T	MGR E SM UM T
Percent with 2 people	39% 86% 83%	31% 91% 81%	50% 97% 50%	37% 65% 50%	30% 84% 100%	56% 83% 100%
Percent with 3 people	9% 9% 10%	13% 5% 8%	6% 0% 50%	0% 20% 50%	19% 14% 0%	11% 13% 0%
Percent with 4 people	6% 2% 5%	0% 3% 8%	11% 0% 0%	7% 10% 0%	11% 0% 0%	0% 0% 0%
Percent with more than 4 people	45% 3% 2%	56% 2% 4%	33% 3% 0%	57% 5% 0%	41% 3% 0%	33% 4% 0%

Appendix B.3
Analysis of Mail Record: Input

Category	Study Composite	Ins. MGR A	Univ. MGR B	Manf. MGR C	Govt. MGR D	Util. MGR E
Number Pieces Received	355	38	61	35	119	102
Form of Input (%)						
Letter	60 16.90%	12 31.58%	14 22.95%	5 14.29%	11 9.24%	18 17.65%
Memo	162 45.63%	17 44.74%	31 50.82%	18 51.43%	72 60.50%	24 23.53%
Report	61 17.18%	5 13.16%	9 14.75%	5 14.29%	20 16.81%	22 21.57%
Periodical	54 15.21%	4 10.53%	2 3.28%	7 20.00%	14 11.76%	27 26.47%
Clipping	13 3.66%	0 .00%	1 1.64%	0 .00%	1 .84%	11 10.78%
Book	5 1.41%	0 .00%	4 6.56%	0 .00%	1 .84%	0 .00%
Attention (%)						
Skim	120 33.80%	12 31.58%	10 16.39%	14 40.00%	36 30.25%	48 47.06%
Read	206 58.03%	19 50.00%	41 67.21%	21 60.00%	79 66.39%	46 45.10%
Study	29 8.17%	7 18.42%	10 16.39%	0 .00%	4 3.36%	8 7.84%

Appendix B.3, continued Analysis of Mail Record: Input						
Category	Study Composite	Ins. MGR A	Univ. MGR B	Manf. MGR C	Govt. MGR D	Util. MGR E
* Sender (%)						
Subordinate	220 61.97%	24 63.16%	33 54.10%	22 57.89%	90 75.63%	51 50.00%
Superior	11 3.10%	1 2.63%	3 4.92%	0 0.00%	4 3.36%	3 2.94%
Peer external	6 1.69%	0 .00%	2 3.28%	0 .00%	1 .84%	3 2.94%
Peer internal	16 4.51%	1 2.63%	3 4.92%	3 7.89%	8 6.72%	1 .98%
Trade Org.	7 1.97%	0 .00%	6 9.84%	0 0.00%	1 .84%	0 .00%
Client	7 1.97%	0 .00%	7 11.48%	0 .00%	0 .00%	0 .00%
Supplier/ vendor	34 9.58%	11 28.95%	2 3.28%	2 5.26%	8 6.72%	11 10.78%
Independent	7 1.97%	0 .00%	2. 3.28%	2 5.26%	2 1.68%	1 .98%
Publisher	45 12.68%	1 2.63%	3 4.92%	7 18.42%	3 2.52%	31 30.39%
Government	5 1.41%	0 .00%	0 .00%	2 5.26%	2 1.68%	1 .98%
Total Senders	35.8	38	61	38	119	102

*   A piece of mail was sometimes from two senders. Therefore, the total
    number of senders exceeds the total pieces of mail. The total number of
    senders was used to analyze percentages from each sender.

Category	Study Composite	Ins.	Univ.	Manf.	Govt. Agency	Util.
		MGR A	MGR B	MGR C	MGR D	MGR E
Purpose of Input Mail (%)						
Acknowledgments	5 1.41%	0 .00%	1 1.64%	0 .00%	1 .84%	3 2.94%
Status requests	3 .85%	0 .00%	0 .00%	1 2.86%	2 1.68%	0 .00%
Solicitations	23 6.48%	11 28.95%	0 .00%	1 2.86%	1 .84%	10 9.80%
Authority requests	95 26.76%	9 23.68%	16 26.23%	17 48.57%	51 42.86%	2 1.96%
Total Requests	126 35.49%	20 52.63%	17 27.87%	19 54.29%	55 46.22%	15 14.71%
Reference data	85 23.94%	7 18.42%	17 27.87%	3 8.57%	35 29.41%	23 22.55%
General reports	15 4.23%	2 5.26%	3 4.92%	4 11.43%	1 .84%	5 4.90%
Periodical news	54 15.21%	3 7.89%	3 4.92%	7 20.00%	16 13.45%	25 24.51%
Events	22 6.20%	0 .00%	1 1.64%	1 2.86%	2 1.68%	18 17.65%
Reports on operations	32 9.01%	4 10.53%	8 13.11%	0 .00%	8 6.72%	12 11.76%
Advice on situations	10 2.82%	1 2.63%	3 4.92%	0 .00%	2 1.68%	4 3.92%
Problems and pressures	6 1.69%	1 2.63%	5 8.20%	0 .00%	0 .00%	0 .00%
Ideas	5 1.41%	0 .00%	4 6.56%	1 2.86%	0 .00%	0 .00%
Total Information	229 64.51%	18 47.37%	44 72.13%	16 45.71%	64 53.78%	87 85.29%

Appendix B.3, continued
Analysis of Mail Record: Input

Appendix B.4
Analysis of Mail Record: Output

CATEGORY	Study Compos- ite	Insur- ance	Univer- sity	Manf.	Govt. Agency	Utilities
		MGR A	MGR B	MGR C	MGR D	MGR E
Number of reac- tions to inputs	35	6	12	1	7	9
Number self-initiated	74	16	33	11	3	11
Total output	109	22	45	12	10	20
Output as a percent of input	30.70%	57.89%	73.77%	34.29%	8.40%	19.61%
Self- initiated as a % of output	67.89%	72.73%	73.33%	91.67%	30.00%	55.00%

FORM OF OUTPUT MAIL (%)	Composite	Insur- ance	Univer- sity	Manf.	Govt. Agency	Utilities
		MGR A	MGR B	MGR C	MGR D	MGR E
Letter	25 22.94%	7 31.82%	7 15.56%	10 83.33%	1 10.00%	0 .00%
Memo	38 34.86%	10 45.45%	15 33.33%	1 8.33%	4 40.00%	8 40.00%
Report	38 34.86%	2 9.09%	21 46.67%	1 8.33%	2 20.00%	12 60.00%
Forwarded letter	4 3.67%	2 9.09%	1 2.22%	0 .00%	1 10.00%	0 .00%
Forwarded memo	1 .92%	0 .00%	1 2.22%	0 .00%	0 .00%	0 .00%
Forwarded other	3 2.75%	1 4.55%	0 .00%	0 .00%	2 20.00%	0 .00%

Appendix B.4, continued
Analysis of Mail Record: Output

CATEGORY	Study Com-posite	Insur-ance	Univer-sity	Manu-facturing	Govt. Agency	Utilities
		MGR A	MGR B	MGR C	MGR D	MGR E
*TARGET (%)						
Subordinate	54 44.63%	17 77.27%	15 32.61%	1 5.56%	8 80.00%	13 52.00%
Superior	22 18.18%	1 4.55%	7 15.22%	7 38.89%	1 10.00%	6 24.00%
Peer external	15 12.40%	0 .00%	15 32.61%	0 .00%	0 .00%	0 .00%
Peer internal	21 17.36%	4 18.18%	4 8.70%	7 38.89%	0 .00%	6 24.00%
Trade org.	4 3.31%	0 .00%	2 4.35%	2 11.11%	0 .00%	0 .00%
Client	1 .83%	0 .00%	1 2.17%	0 .00%	0 .00%	0 .00%
Supplier or vendor	3 2.48%	0 .00%	1 2.17%	1 5.56%	1 10.00%	0 .00%
Independent	1 .83%	0 .00%	12 .17%	0 .00%	0 .00%	0 .00%
Government	0 .00%	0 .00%	0 .00%	0 .00%	0 .00%	0 .00%
Total Targets	121	22	46	18	10	25

Appendix B.4, continued
Analysis of Mail Record: Output

PURPOSE OF OUTPUT MAIL (%)	Study Composite	Insurance	University	Manufacturing	Govt. Agency	Utilities
		MRG A	MGR B	MGR C	MGR D	MGR E
Acknowledgment input	0 .00%	0 .00%	.00%	.00%	.00%	0 .00%
Reply to written requests	12 11.01%	1 4.55%	9 20.00%	.00%	1 10.00%	1 5.00%
Reply to information received	9 8.26%	0 .00%	5 11.11%	1 8.33%	.00%	3 15.00%
Forward information to subordinates	20 18.35%	5 22.73%	4 8.89%	.00%	7 70.00%	4 20 00%
Forward request to subordinates	4 3.67%	2 9.09%	.00%	1 8.33%	.00%	1 5.00%
Write to 3rd party re input	3 2.75%	1 4.55%	1 2.22%	.00%	.00%	1 5.00%
Acknowledge/reply to verbal contact	2 1.83%	0 .00%	1 2.22%	1 8.33%	.00%	0 .00%
Write report	31 28.44%	2 9.09%	18 40.00%	1 8.33%	1 10.00%	9 45.00%
Originate letter or memo	28 25.69%	11 50.00%	7 15.56%	8 66.67%	1 10.00%	1 5.00%

*Mail sometimes had more than one target. Therefore, the total number of targets exceeded the total pieces of mail. The total number of targets was used to analyze percentages from each sender.

Appendix B.5
Analysis of Mail Record: Input (Attention)

CATEGORY	Study Composite	Insur-ance	Univer-sity	Manufactur-ing	Govt. Agency	Utilities
		MRG A	MRG B	MRG C	MRG D	MRG E
Number Pieces Received	355	38	61	35	119	102
FORM OF INPUT (%)						
Letter	60 16.90%	12 31.58%	14 22.95%	5 14.29%	11 9.24%	18 17.65%
Memo	162 45.63%	17 44.74%	31 50.82%	18 51.43%	72 60.50%	24 23.53%
Report	61 17.18%	5 13.16%	9 14.75%	5 14.29%	20 16.81%	22 21.57%
Periodical	54 15.21%	4 10.53%	2 3.28%	7 20.00%	14 11.76%	27 26.47%
Clipping	13 3.66%	0 .00%	1 1.64%	0 .00%	1 .84%	11 10.78%
Book	5 1.41%	0 .00%	4 6.56%	0 .00%	1 .84%	0 .00%

ATTENTION (%)						
	Compos-ite	Insurance	Univer-sity	Manf.	Govt.	Utilities
Skim	255 71.83%	23 60.53%	36 59.02%	32 91.43%	98 82.35%	66 64.71%
Read	71 20.00%	8 21.05%	15 24.59%	3 8.57%	17 14.29%	28 27.45%
Study	29 8.17%	7 18.42%	10 16.39%	0 .00%	4 3.36%	8 7.84%

Appendix B.5, continued
Analysis of Mail Record: Input (Attention)

CATEGORY	Study Composite	Insurance	University	Manufac-turing	Govt. Agency	Utilities
		MRG A	MRG B	MRG C	MRG D	MRG E
*SENDER (%)						
Subordinate	220 61.97%	24 63.16%	33 54.10%	22 57.89%	90 75.63%	51 50.00%
Superior	11 3.10%	1 2.63%	3 4.92%	0 .00%	4 3.36%	3 2.94%
Peer external	6 1.69%	0 .00%	2 3.28%	0 .00%	1 .84%	3 2.94%
Peer internal	16 4.51%	1 2.63%	3 4.92%	3 7.89%	8 6.72%	1 .98%
Trade organization	7 1.97%	0 .00%	6 9.84%	0 .00%	1 .84%	0 .00%
Client	7 1.97%	0 .00%	7 11.48%	0 .00%	0 .00%	0 .00%
Supplier or vendor	34 9.58%	11 28.95%	2 3.28%	2 5.26%	8 6.72%	11 10.78%
Independent	7 1.97%	0 .00%	2 3.28%	2 5.26%	2 1.68%	1 .98%
Publisher	45 12.68%	1 2.63%	3 4.92%	7 18.42%	3 2.52%	31 30.39%
Government	5 1.41%	0 .00%	0 .00%	2 5.26%	2 1.68%	1 .98%
Total Senders	358	38	61	38	119	102

*A piece of mail was sometimes from two senders. Therefore, the total number of senders exceeds the total pieces of mail. The total number of senders was used to analyze percentages from each sender.

Appendix B.5, continued
Analysis of Mail Record: Input (Attention)

PURPOSE OF INPUT MAIL (%)	Study Composite	Insurance	University	Manufacturing	Govt. Agency	Utilities
		MGR A	MGR B	MGR C	MGR D	MRG E
Acknowledgments	5 1.41%	0 .00%	1 1.64%	0 .00%	1 .84%	3 2.94%
Status requests	3 .85%	0 .00%	0 .00%	1 2.86%	2 1.68%	0 .00%
Solicitations	23 6.48%	11 28.95%	0 .00%	1 2.86%	1 .84%	10 9.80%
Authority requests	95 26.76%	9 23.68%	16 26.23%	17 48.57%	51 42.86%	2 1.96%
Total Requests	126 35.49%	20 52.63%	17 27.87%	19 54.29%	55 46.22%	15 14.71%
Reference data	85 23.94%	7 18.42%	17 27.87%	3 8.57%	35 29.41%	23 22.55%
General reports	15 4.23%	2 5.26%	3 4.92%	4 11.43%	1 .84%	5 4.90%
Periodical news	54 15.21%	3 7.89%	3 4.92%	7 20.00%	16 13.45%	25 24.51%
Events	22 6.20%	0 .00%	1 1.64%	1 2.86%	2 1.68%	18 17.65%
Reports on operations	32 9.01%	4 10.53%	8 13.11%	0 .00%	8 6.72%	12 11.76%
Advice on situations	10 2.82%	1 2.63%	3 4.92%	0 .00%	2 1.68%	4 3.92%
Problems and pressures	6 1.69%	1 2.63%	5 8.20%	0 .00%	0 .00%	0 .00%
Ideas	5 1.41%	0 .00%	4 6.56%	1 2.86%	0 .00%	0 .00%
Total Information	229 64.51%	18 47.37%	44 72.13%	16 45.71%	64 53.78%	87 85.29%

Appendix B.6
Analysis of Mintzberg's Verbal Purpose Subcategories
(Minutes for Each Subcategory)

Purpose Code	Total Minutes	Ins. Mgr. A	Univ. Mgr. B	Mfg. Mgr. C	Govt. Mgr. D	Util. Mgr. E
22	57				57	
23	491	47	181	140	73	50
24	434	121	110	15	50	138
25	160	0		160		
26	126	22	2	40	40	22
27a	127	34	15	4	70	4
27b	62	15	30		5	12
27c	0					
27d	230	35	93	96	6	
28a	110	13	42		31	24
28b	84	54	6	2	19	3
28c	121	32	21		37	31
29	47	47				
30a	47	15	26	2		4
30b	530	69	67	55	69	270
30c	643	376	53	47	167	
31a	110	44	23	5	33	5
31b	280	119	9		150	2
31c	381	50	29	298		4
32a	1705	410	341	538	232	184
32b	48		45	3		
32c	362	15	6	297	16	28
32d	0					
32e	88		11		37	40
32f	0					
33a	855		33	292	109	421
33b	184		77	92	15	
33c	578	122	153	180	80	43
33d	1231	390			367	474
34	237		87		150	
	9328	2030	1460	2266	1813	1759

Appendix B.6, continued
Analysis of Mintzberg's Verbal Purpose Subcategories
(Percent of Verbal Contact Time)

Purpose Code	Avg. % time	Ins. Mgr. A	Univ. Mgr. B	Mfg. Mgr. C	Govt. Mgr. D	Util. Mgr. E
22	1%	0%	0%	0%	3%	0%
23	5%	2%	12%	6%	4%	3%
24	5%	6%	8%	1%	3%	8%
25	2%	0%	0%	7%	0%	0%
26	1%	1%	0%	2%	2%	1%
27a	1%	2%	1%	0%	4%	0%
27b	1%	1%	2%	0%	0%	1%
27c	0%	0%	0%	0%	0%	0%
27d	2%	2%	6%	4%	0%	0%
28a	1%	1%	3%	0%	2%	1%
28b	1%	3%	0%	0%	1%	0%
28c	1%	2%	1%	0%	2%	2%
29	1%	2%	0%	0%	0%	0%
30a	1%	1%	2%	0%	0%	0%
30b	6%	3%	5%	2%	4%	15%
30c	7%	19%	4%	2%	9%	0%
31a	1%	2%	2%	0%	2%	0%
31b	3%	6%	1%	0%	8%	0%
31c	4%	2%	2%	13%	0%	0%
32a	18%	20%	23%	24%	13%	10%
32b	1%	0%	3%	0%	0%	0%
32c	4%	1%	0%	13%	1%	2%
32d	0%	0%	0%	0%	0%	0%
32e	1%	0%	1%	0%	2%	2%
32f	0%	0%	0%	0%	0%	0%
33a	9%	0%	2%	13%	6%	24%
33b	2%	0%	5%	4%	1%	0%
33c	6%	6%	10%	8%	4%	2%
33d	13%	19%	0%	0%	20%	27%
34	3%	0%	6%	0%	8%	0%
	100%	100%	100%	100%	100%	100%

Appendix B.6, continued
Analysis of Mintzberg's Verbal Purpose Subcategories
(Number of Occurrences)

Purpose Code	Total occ's.	Ins. Mgr. A	Univ. Mgr. B	Mfg. Mgr. C	Govt. Mgr. D	Util. Mgr. E
22	1				1	
23	66	14	10	17	14	11
24	24	3	4	3	2	12
25	2	0		2		
26	15	3	1	2	2	7
27a	23	5	1	2	14	1
27b	11	2	3		1	5
27c	0		0			
27d	16	4	7	3	2	
28a	23	4	5		9	5
28b	16	8	1	1	5	1
28c	25	4	5		7	9
29	12	12				
30a	6	2	2	1		1
30b	22	11	3	3	3	2
30c	15	7	5	2	1	
31a	17	7	1	1	7	1
31b	23	10	2		10	1
31c	17	5	4	7		1
32a	74	23	15	17	10	9
32b	2		1	1		
32c	14	1	1	7	3	2
32d	0					
32e	6		1		3	2
32f	0					
33a	19		1	3	2	13
33b	4		1	2	1	
33c	25	2	7	8	7	1
33d	18	2			9	7
34	5		1		4	
	501	129	82	82	117	91

Appendix B.6, continued
Analysis of Mintzberg's Verbal Purpose Subcategories
(Percent of Verbal Contact Occurrences)

Purpose Code	Avg. % occ.	Ins. Mgr. A	Univ. Mgr. B	Mfg. Mgr. C	Govt. Mgr. D	Util. Mgr. E
22	0%	0%	0%	0%	1%	0%
23	13%	11%	12%	21%	12%	12%
24	5%	2%	5%	4%	2%	13%
25	0%	0%	0%	2%	0%	0%
26	3%	2%	1%	2%	2%	8%
27a	5%	4%	1%	2%	12%	1%
27b	2%	2%	4%	0%	1%	5%
27c	0%	0%	0%	0%	0%	0%
27d	3%	3%	9%	4%	2%	0%
28a	5%	3%	6%	0%	8%	5%
28b	3%	6%	1%	1%	4%	1%
28c	5%	3%	6%	0%	6%	10%
29	2%	9%	0%	0%	0%	0%
30a	1%	2%	2%	1%	0%	1%
30b	4%	9%	4%	4%	3%	2%
30c	3%	5%	6%	2%	1%	0%
31a	3%	5%	1%	1%	6%	1%
31b	5%	8%	2%	0%	9%	1%
31c	3%	4%	5%	9%	0%	1%
32a	15%	18%	18%	21%	9%	10%
32b	0%	0%	1%	1%	0%	0%
32c	3%	1%	1%	9%	3%	2%
32d	0%	0%	0%	0%	0%	0%
32e	1%	0%	1%	0%	3%	2%
32f	0%	0%	0%	0%	0%	0%
33a	4%	0%	1%	4%	2%	14%
33b	1%	0%	1%	2%	1%	0%
33c	5%	2%	9%	10%	6%	1%
33d	4%	2%	0%	0%	8%	8%
34	1%	0%	1%	0%	3%	0%
	100%	100%	100%	100%	100%	100%

Appendix B.7
Analysis of Mintzberg's Incoming Desk Work Purpose Subcategories

(Number of Occurrences)

Purpose Code	Total occ's.	Ins. Mgr A	Univ. Mgr B	Mfg. Mgr C	Govt. Mgr D	Util. Mgr E
1	5		1		1	3
2a	0					
2b	3			1	2	
2c	0					
3	13	11		1	1	
4a	4				4	
4b	15	3	1	3	8	
4c	76	6	15	14	39	2
5a	73	7	11	2	32	21
5b	5		2		1	2
5c	6		3	1	2	
6a	9	1	3	2		3
6b	6	1		2	1	2
7a	2			1		1
7b	7	1	1		3	2
7c	7		1	5		1
7d	11			1		10
7e	2					2
7f	11	1			4	6
7g	13		1		9	3
8a	13		1	1		11
8b	6				2	4
8c	1					1
8d	2					2
8e	0					
9a	17	2			7	8
9b	14	2	8		1	3
9c	1					1
10	10	1	3		2	4
11	5		5			
12	5		4	1		
	342	36	60	35	119	92

Appendix B.7, continued
Analysis of Mintzberg's Incoming Desk Work Purpose
Subcategories
(Percent of Occurrences)

Purpose Code	Avg. % occ.	Ins. Mgr. A	Univ. Mgr. B	Mfg. Mgr. C	Govt. Mgr. D	Util. Mgr. E
1	1%	0%	2%	0%	1%	3%
2a	0%	0%	0%	0%	0%	0%
2b	1%	0%	0%	3%	2%	0%
2c	0%	0%	0%	0%	0%	0%
3	4%	31%	0%	3%	1%	0%
4a	1%	0%	0%	0%	3%	0%
4b	4%	8%	2%	9%	7%	0%
4c	22%	17%	25%	40%	33%	2%
5a	21%	19%	18%	6%	27%	23%
5b	1%	0%	3%	0%	1%	2%
5c	2%	0%	5%	3%	2%	0%
6a	3%	3%	5%	6%	0%	3%
6b	2%	3%	0%	6%	1%	2%
7a	1%	0%	0%	3%	0%	1%
7b	2%	3%	2%	0%	3%	2%
7c	2%	0%	2%	14%	0%	1%
7d	3%	0%	0%	3%	0%	11%
7e	1%	0%	0%	0%	0%	2%
7f	3%	3%	0%	0%	3%	7%
7g	4%	0%	2%	0%	8%	3%
8a	4%	0%	2%	3%	0%	12%
8b	2%	0%	0%	0%	2%	4%
8c	0%	0%	0%	0%	0%	1%
8d	1%	0%	0%	0%	0%	2%
8e	0%	0%	0%	0%	0%	0%
9a	5%	6%	0%	0%	6%	9%
9b	4%	6%	13%	0%	1%	3%
9c	0%	0%	0%	0%	0%	1%
10	3%	3%	5%	0%	2%	4%
11	1%	0%	8%	0%	0%	0%
12	1%	0%	7%	3%	0%	0%
	100%	100%	100%	100%	100%	100%

Appendix C:

Frequency Duration

Appendix C.1
Frequency Duration for All Activities

DURATION	COMPOS-ITE	RANGE		Ins	Univ	Mfg	Govt	Util
Minutes	Occurrences	MIN/ MAX		Mgr A	Mgr B	Mgr C	Mgr D	Mgr E
1	37	0	18	18	4	0	9	6
2	92	11	22	18	11	20	22	21
3	56	41	8	14	4	5	18	15
4	28	0	9	6	6	0	7	9
5	74	9	20	20	15	9	17	13
6	16	0	6	6	6	0	1	3
7	12	0	5	1	4	0	2	5
8	23	2	8	8	4	5	4	2
9	15	3	3	3	3	3	3	3
10	38	2	11	10	9	6	11	2
11	7	0	4	2	1	4		0
12	9	1	4	1	1	3		4
13	8	0	7		7	0		1
14	11	1	4	2	4	1	3	1
15	17	1	10	10	2	1	2	2
16	5	0	3		3	1	1	0
17	6	0	2		2	0	2	2
18	3	0	2	1		2	0	
19	7	1	3	2	1	1	3	
20	14	1	4	3	1	3	4	3
21-30	27	2	8	7	5	2	5	8
31-50	46	3	14	3	11	8	14	10
51-70	24	3	7	7	3	6	4	4
71-90	16	1	7	1	3	4	1	7
91-120	20	3	7	4	3	7	3	3
>120	12	1	5	1	5	3	1	2
Total	623	94	148	148	118	94	137	126
% 30 mins or less	81%	70%	89%	89%	79%	70%	83%	79%
% 20 mins or less	77%	68%	84%	84%	75%	68%	80%	73%
% 15 mins or less	71%	61%	80%	80%	69%	61%	72%	69%
% 10 mins or less	63%	51%	70%	70%	56%	51%	69%	63%
% 5 mins or less	46%	34%	53%	51%	34%	36%	53%	51%

Appendix D:

Extended Mail Analysis

Appendix D.1
Area for Mail: Percent of Total Pieces of Mail

AREA	STUDY COM- POSITE	RANGE		Ins Mgr A	Univ Mgr B	Mfg Mgr C	Govt Mgr D	Util Mgr E
External	28%	16%	40%	20%	33%	34%	16%	40%
Functional	26%	19%	38%	22%	30%	38%	27%	19%
Mix	2%	0%	19%	0%	0%	19%	1%	0%
Subtotal other than IT	57%	42%	91%	42%	63%	91%	43%	59%
Information Technology	43%	9%	58%	58%	37%	9%	57%	41%

Appendix D.2
Location of Desk Work: Percent of Mail by Location

AREA	STUDY COM- POSITE	Ins Mgr A	Univ Mgr B	Mfg Mgr C	Govt Mgr D	Util Mgr E
Manager's Office	78%	92%	75%	4%	99%	81%
Other than manager's office	22%	9%	25%	96%	1%	19%
Office of subordinate	4%	7%	0%	34%	0%	0%
Office of superior	0%	0%	1%	0%	0%	0%
Hall or plant	0%	0%	0%	0%	0%	0%
Conference or board room	1%	2%	0%	9%	0%	0%
Away from organization	8%	0%	3%	30%	0%	17%
Peer's office	0%	0%	0%	0%	0%	0%
Home	8%	1%	21%	23%	1%	2%

Appendix D.3
Extended Analysis of Mail Form
(Number of occurrences)

Form Code	Total # of occ's	Ins. Mgr. A	Univ. Mgr. B	Mfg. Mgr. C	Govt. Mgr. D	Util. Mgr. E
A	18				15	3
AE	4				3	1
AF	67	6		17	44	
B	5		4		1	
CL	13		1		1	11
L	53	11	10	5	11	16
LE	7	1	4			2
M	23	3	5	1	7	7
ME	50	8	26		3	13
P	52	4	2	7	14	25
PE	2					2
R	55	5	9	5	20	16
RE	6					6
	355	38	61	35	119	102

(Percent of occurrences)

Form Code	Avg. % occ's	Ins. Mgr. A	Univ. Mgr. B	Mfg. Mgr. C	Govt. Mgr. D	Util. Mgr. E
A	5%	0%	0%	0%	13%	3%
AE	1%	0%	0%	0%	3%	1%
AF	19%	16%	0%	49%	37%	0%
B	1%	0%	7%	0%	1%	0%
CL	4%	0%	2%	0%	1%	11%
L	15%	29%	16%	14%	9%	16%
LE	2%	3%	7%	0%	0%	2%
M	6%	8%	8%	3%	6%	7%
ME	14%	21%	43%	0%	3%	13%
P	15%	11%	3%	20%	12%	25%
PE	1%	0%	0%	0%	0%	2%
R	15%	13%	15%	14%	17%	16%
RE	2%	0%	0%	0%	0%	6%
	100%	100%	100%	100%	100%	100%

Appendix E:

Responsibility Analysis

Appendix E.1
Verbal Contacts: Percent of Occurrences

Area	Com-posite	Range		Ins Mgr A	Univ Mgr B	Mfg Mgr C	Govt Mgr D	Util Mgr E
Policies, procedures, guidelines	6%	1%	13%	2%	13%	1%	10%	3%
Strategic planning	16%	7%	36%	7%	12%	22%	7%	35%
Approval, acceptance of expenditure	20%	9%	35%	19%	9%	15%	35%	15%
Coordination of 3 groups (IT, F, E)	24%	17%	29%	28%	17%	22%	24%	29%
Education	1%	0%	6%	1%	0%	6%	1%	0%
Consulting (present problems)	10%	0%	18%	7%	17%	18%	9%	0%
Other general managerial	21%	14%	33%	33%	24%	15%	14%	16%
Environmental scanning	2%	0%	7%	3%	7%	1%	0%	0%

Appendix E.1, continued
Verbal Contacts: Percent of Time

Area	Com-posite	Range		Ins Mgr A	Univ Mgr B	Mfg Mgr C	Govt Mgr D	Util Mgr E
Policies, procedures, guidelines	7%	0%	20%	4%	11%	0%	20%	0%
Strategic planning	35%	4%	73%	43%	14%	36%	4%	73%
Approval, acceptance of expenditure	10%	3%	25%	8%	6%	10%	25%	3%
Coordination of 3 groups (IT, F, E)	21%	18%	27%	19%	25%	18%	27%	20%
Education	4%	0%	9%	0%	0%	8%	9%	0%
Consulting (present problems)	10%	0%	24%	3%	15%	24%	6%	0%
Other general managerial	10%	3%	21%	21%	16%	3%	9%	4%
Environmental scanning	2%	0%	12%	2%	12%	0%	0%	0%

Appendix E.2
Comparison of Verbal and Nonverbal Medium

AREA	% of occurrences		% of time Verbal
	Desk Work	Verbal	
Policies, procedures, guidelines	7%	6%	7%
Strategic planning	9%	16%	35%
Approval, acceptance of expenditure	25%	20%	10%
Coordination of 3 groups (IT, F, E)	23%	24%	21%
Education			
Consulting (present problems)	1%	1%	4%
Other general managerial	2%	10%	10%
Environmental scanning	14%	21%	10%
	20%	2%	2%

Appendix E.3
Desk Work: Percent of Occurrences

Area	Com-posite	Range		Ins Mgr A	Univ Mgr B	Mfg Mgr C	Govt Mgr D	Util Mgr E
Policies, procedures, guidelines	7%	3%	12%	12%	10%	11%	4%	3%
Strategic planning	9%	2%	17%	7%	13%	17%	2%	9%
Approval, acceptance of expenditure	25%	8%	45%	32%	9%	45%	42%	8%
Coordination of 3 groups (IT, F, E)	23%	6%	27%	22%	25%	6%	24%	27%
Education	1%	0%	3%	0%	3%	0%	0%	1%
Consulting (present problems)	2%	0%	8%	0%	8%	0%	0%	0%
Other general managerial	14%	6%	19%	15%	13%	6%	19%	11%
Environmental scanning	20%	9%	40%	13%	18%	15%	9%	40%

Appendix E.4
All Mail and Contacts: Percent of Occurrences

Area	Com-posite	Range		Ins Mgr A	Univ Mgr B	Mfg Mgr C	Govt Mgr D	Util Mgr E
Policies, procedures, guidelines	6%	3%	12%	5%	12%	5%	7%	3%
Strategic planning	12%	4%	21%	7%	13%	20%	4%	21%
Approval, acceptance of expenditure	22%	9%	39%	23%	9%	26%	39%	11%
Coordination of 3 groups (IT, F, E)	24%	16%	28%	26%	22%	16%	24%	28%
Education	1%	0%	4%	1%	2%	4%	0%	0%
Consulting (present problems)	6%	0%	12%	5%	12%	12%	4%	0%
Other general managerial	18%	12%	27%	27%	18%	12%	16%	14%
Environmental scanning	11%	5%	23%	6%	13%	6%	5%	23%

Appendix F:

Roles Analysis

Appendix F.1
Verbal: Percent of Occurrences

ROLE	All	Range		Ins Mgr A	Univ Mgr B	Mfg Mgr C	Govt Mgr D	Util Mgr E
Figurehead	6%	4%	13%	5%	4%	4%	4%	13%
Monitor	11%	2%	20%	18%	7%	20%	2%	7%
Disseminator	10%	2%	16%	16%	6%	2%	10%	10%
Spokesman	7%	6%	9%	6%	6%	7%	8%	9%
Entrepreneur	6%	3%	7%	7%	7%	6%	7%	3%
Disturbance Handler	20%	8%	40%	18%	40%	15%	20%	8%
Resource Allocator	39%	28%	49%	30%	28%	45%	49%	41%
Negotiator	3%	1%	10%	1%	1%	1%	1%	10%
ROLE GROUPS:*								
Information	27%	20%	40%	40%	20%	29%	20%	25%
Decisional	67%	56%	77%	56%	77%	67%	76%	62%

*The only Interpersonal role which could be used for the analysis is Figurehead. All activities were coded with one of the other two Interpersonal roles, Leader or Liaison.

Appendix F.1, continued
Verbal: Percent of Time

ROLE	All	Range	Ins	Univ	Mfg	Govt	Util
Figurehead	5%	1% 8%	6%	7%	1%	6%	8%
Monitor	12%	3% 30%	13%	4%	30%	3%	3%
Disseminator	9%	4% 14%	10%	4%	5%	14%	10%
Spokesman	5%	2% 10%	2%	2%	4%	10%	5%
Entrepreneur	18%	5% 39%	39%	18%	14%	14%	5%
Disturbance Handler	16%	1% 45%	8%	45%	19%	14%	1%
Resource Allocator	30%	14% 52%	21%	14%	23%	38%	52%
Negotiator	5%	0% 16%	0%	6%	3%	0%	16%
ROLE GROUPS:*							
Information	25%	10% 40%	25%	10%	40%	27%	18%
Decisional Roles	69%	59% 83%	69%	83%	59%	66%	74%

*The only Interpersonal role which could be used for the analysis is Figurehead. All activities were coded with one of the other two interpersonal roles, Leader or Liaison.

Appendix F.2
Scheduled Meetings: Percent of Occurrences

ROLE	All	Range		Ins	Univ	Mfg	Govt	Util
Figurehead	5%	0%	11%	6%	11%	0%	4%	6%
Monitor	9%	0%	30%	6%	0%	30%	0%	0%
Disseminator	6%	3%	11%	6%	6%	3%	11%	6%
Spokesman	5%	0%	11%	0%	0%	3%	11%	6%
Entrepreneur	17%	6%	50%	50%	22%	10%	7%	6%
Disturbance Handler	15%	0%	44%	6%	44%	17%	7%	0%
Resource Allocator	39%	11%	56%	25%	11%	37%	56%	56%
Negotiator	6%	0%	22%	0%	6%	0%	4%	22%
ROLE GROUP:*								
Information	20%	6%	37%	13%	6%	37%	22%	11%
Decisional	75%	63%	83%	81%	83%	63%	74%	83%

*The only Interpersonal role which could be used for the analysis is Figurehead. All activities were coded with one of the other two Interpersonal roles, Leader or Liaison

Appendix F.2, continued
Scheduled Meetings: Percent of Time

ROLE	All	Range		Ins	Univ	Mfg	Govt	Util
Figurehead	6%	0%	10%	10%	9%	0%	4%	9%
Monitor	11%	0%	41%	6%	0%	41%	0%	0%
Disseminator	8%	5%	19%	5%	5%	6%	19%	7%
Spokesman	5%	0%	13%	0%	0%	4%	13%	5%
Entrepreneur	25%	6%	68%	68%	24%	16%	15%	6%
Disturbance Handler	13%	0%	47%	1%	47%	13%	8%	0%
Resource Allocator	27%	6%	55%	10%	6%	21%	39%	55%
Negotiator	6%	0%	19%	0%	9%	0%	1%	19%
ROLE GROUP:*								
Information	24%	5%	51%	11%	5%	51%	32%	12%
Decisional	70%	49%	86%	79%	86%	49%	63%	80%

*The only Interpersonal role which could be used for the analysis is Figurehead. All
activities were coded with one of the other two interpersonal roles, Leader or Liaison.

Appendix F.3
Unscheduled Meetings: Percent of Occurrences

ROLE	All	Range	Ins	Univ	Mfg	Govt	Util
Figurehead	2%	0% 5%	2%	0%	0%	5%	0%
Monitor	13%	0% 18%	18%	10%	15%	0%	17%
Disseminator	13%	5% 20%	20%	7%	5%	8%	13%
Spokesman	10%	3% 20%	11%	3%	20%	5%	13%
Entrepreneur	5%	2% 11%	2%	7%	5%	11%	4%
Disturbance Handler	25%	10% 50%	24%	50%	10%	19%	17%
Resource Allocator	33%	23% 51%	24%	23%	45%	51%	30%
Negotiator	1%	0% 4%	0%	0%	0%	0%	4%
ROLE GROUP:*							
Information	35%	14% 48%	48%	20%	40%	14%	43%
Decisional	64%	50% 81%	50%	80%	60%	81%	57%

*The only Interpersonal role which could be used for the analysis is Figurehead. All
activities were coded with one of the other two Interpersonal roles, Leader or Liaison

Appendix F.3, continued
Unscheduled Meetings: Percent of Time

ROLE	All	Range		Ins	Univ	Mfg	Govt	Util
Figurehead	4%	0%	19%	1%	0%	0%	19%	0%
Monitor	14%	0%	22%	22%	14%	9%	0%	16%
Disseminator	10%	2%	17%	17%	2%	8%	3%	15%
Spokesman	5%	3%	6%	6%	6%	6%	3%	4%
Entrepreneur	9%	0%	20%	0%	11%	18%	20%	2%
Disturbance Handler	24%	5%	49%	21%	49%	32%	17%	5%
Resource Allocator	34%	18%	56%	33%	18%	26%	38%	56%
Negotiator	0%	0%	2%	0%	0%	0%	0%	2%
ROLE GROUP:*								
Information	30%	6%	45%	45%	22%	24%	6%	35%
Decisional	67%	54%	78%	54%	78%	76%	75%	65%

*The only Interpersonal role which could be used for the analysis is Figurehead. All activities were coded with one of the other two Interpersonal roles, Leader or Liaison.

Appendix F.4, continued
Calls: Percent of Occurrences

ROLE	All	Range	Ins	Univ	Mfg	Govt	Util
Figurehead	2%	0% 5%	5%	0%	3%	2%	3%
Monitor	6%	0% 13%	0%	9%	13%	4%	5%
Disseminator	10%	0% 19%	19%	6%	0%	12%	13%
Spokesman	8%	3% 13%	5%	13%	3%	8%	10%
Entrepreneur	2%	0% 4%	0%	0%	3%	4%	3%
Disturbance Handler	21%	8% 31%	19%	31%	17%	27%	8%
Resource Allocator	47%	41% 57%	48%	41%	57%	43%	50%
Negotiator	3%	0% 10%	5%	0%	3%	0%	10%
ROLE GROUP:*							
Information	24%	17% 28%	24%	28%	17%	24%	28%
Decisional	74%	70% 80%	71%	72%	80%	75%	70%

*The only Interpersonal role which could be used for the analysis is Figurehead. All activities were coded with one of the other two Interpersonal roles, Leader or Liaison.

Appendix F.4, continued
Calls: Percent of Time

ROLE	All	Range	Ins	Univ	Mfg	Govt	Util
Figurehead	1%	0% 4%	4%	0%	1%	1%	1%
Monitor	9%	0% 15%	0%	10%	6%	15%	5%
Disseminator	8%	0% 27%	15%	3%	0%	9%	27%
Spokesman	6%	3% 11%	3%	11%	3%	6%	9%
Entrepreneur	1%	0% 3%	0%	0%	1%	2%	3%
Disturbance Handler	28%	3% 35%	15%	35%	35%	34%	3%
Resource Allocator	36%	33% 54%	54%	41%	33%	34%	36%
Negotiator	10%	0% 21%	8%	0%	21%	0%	17%
ROLE GROUP:*							
Information	23%	10% 40%	18%	24%	10%	29%	40%
Decisional	75%	59% 89%	77%	76%	89%	69%	59%

*The only Interpersonal role which could be used for the analysis is Figurehead. All activities were coded with one of the other two Interpersonal roles, Leader or Liaison.

Appendix F.5
Desk Work

ROLE	All	Range	Ins	Univ	Mfg	Govt	Util
Figurehead	2%	0% 5%	2%	1%	0%	2%	5%
Monitor	30%	14% 61%	20%	14%	23%	20%	61%
Disseminator	6%	0% 22%	22%	5%	0%	9%	1%
Spokesman	9%	4% 15%	7%	10%	6%	15%	4%
Entrepreneur	11%	3% 26%	7%	26%	15%	3%	7%
Disturbance Handler	5%	2% 14%	3%	14%	4%	3%	2%
Resource Allocator	35%	20% 49%	40%	29%	49%	48%	20%
Negotiator	0%	0% 2%	0%	0%	2%	1%	0%
ROLE GROUP:*							
Information	45%	29% 66%	48%	29%	30%	43%	66%
Decisional	52%	29% 70%	50%	70%	70%	55%	29%

*The only Interpersonal role which could be used for the analysis is Figurehead. All activities were coded with one of the other two Interpersonal roles, Leader or Liaison.

Appendix F.6
Desk Work In

ROLE	All	Range	Ins	Univ	Mfg	Govt	Util
Figurehead	2%	0% 4%	0%	2%	0%	2%	4%
Monitor	36%	19% 70%	29%	21%	31%	19%	70%
Disseminator	4%	0% 8%	5%	3%	0%	8%	0%
Spokesman	6%	0% 14%	5%	7%	0%	14%	0%
Entrepreneur	6%	3% 15%	3%	15%	3%	3%	7%
Disturbance Handler	6%	2% 20%	5%	20%	3%	3%	2%
Resource Allocator	39%	18% 63%	53%	33%	63%	50%	18%
Negotiator	0%	0% 1%	0%	0%	0%	1%	0%
ROLE GROUP:*							
Information	46%	31% 70%	39%	31%	31%	41%	70%
Decisional	52%	26% 69%	61%	67%	69%	57%	26%

*The only Interpersonal role which could be used for the analysis is Figurehead. All activities were coded with one of the other two Interpersonal roles, Leader or Liaison.

Appendix F.7
Desk Work Out

ROLE	All	Range		Ins	Univ	Mfg	Govt	Util
Figurehead	3%	0%	10%	5%	0%	0%	0%	10%
Monitor	9%	0%	30%	5%	4%	0%	30%	20%
Disseminator	16%	0%	50%	50%	7%	0%	20%	5%
Spokesman	17%	9%	25%	9%	16%	25%	20%	25%
Entrepreneur	28%	0%	50%	14%	42%	50%	0%	10%
Disturbance Handler	4%	0%	8%	0%	7%	8%	0%	0%
Resource Allocator	23%	8%	30%	18%	24%	8%	30%	30%
Negotiator	1%	0%	8%	0%	0%	8%	0%	0%
ROLE GROUP:*								
Information	42%	25%	70%	64%	27%	25%	70%	50%
Decisional	55%	30%	75%	32%	73%	75%	30%	40%

*The only Interpersonal role which could be used for the analysis is Figurehead. All activities were coded with one of the other two Interpersonal roles, Leader or Liaison.

Appendix F.8
Percent of Mail and Contacts

ROLE	All	Range	Ins	Univ	Mfg	Govt	Util
Figurehead	4%	2% 8%	4%	2%	2%	3%	8%
Monitor	20%	11% 38%	19%	11%	21%	11%	38%
Disseminator	8%	2% 17%	17%	5%	2%	9%	5%
Spokesman	8%	6% 11%	6%	9%	7%	11%	6%
Entrepreneur	9%	5% 18%	7%	18%	9%	5%	6%
Disturbance Handler	13%	4% 26%	13%	26%	11%	11%	4%
Resource Allocator	37%	29% 48%	33%	29%	47%	48%	29%
Negotiator	2%	1% 4%	1%	1%	2%	1%	4%
ROLE GROUP:*							
Information	36%	25% 49%	42%	25%	29%	32%	49%
Decisional	60%	43% 73%	54%	73%	68%	65%	43%

*The only Interpersonal role which could be used for the analysis is Figurehead. All activities were coded with one of the other two Interpersonal roles, Leader or Liaison.

Appendix F.9
Comparison of Verbal and Nonverbal: Desk work

	In	Out	Total	Verbal		SM	UM	C
Role	% of Occurrences			%of Occ.	% of Time	% of Time		
Figurehead	2%	3%	2%	6%	5%	6%	4%	1%
Monitor	36%	9%	30%	11%	12%	11%	14%	9%
Disseminator	4%	16%	6%	10%	9%	8%	10%	8%
Spokesman	6%	17%	9%	7%	5%	5%	5%	6%
Entrepreneur	6%	28%	11%	6%	18%	25%	9%	1%
Disturbance Handler	6%	4%	5%	20%	16%	13%	24%	28%
Resource Allocator	39%	23%	35%	39%	30%	27%	34%	36%
Negotiator	0%	1%	0%	3%	5%	6%	0%	10%

Appendix G:

Comparison with Mintzberg

Appendix G.1
Comparison with Chronology Record

CATEGORY	STUDY COMPOSITE	MINTZBERG'S COMPOSITE	STUDY RANGE		MINTZBERG'S RANGE	
*Total hours worked	215	202	35	50	28	53
*Hours in travel (not included)	7	18	0	3.0	.3	7.1
Hours of evening meetings	5	24	0	4.5	0	11
Total amount of mail	464	890	47	129	112	230
Avg mail processed/day	19	36	9	26	22	46
Total number of activities	623	547	94	148	86	160
DESK WORK:						
No. of sessions	122	179	12	36	25	54
Time on desk work (hours)	59	44	5.3	25.3	6.4	10.7
Average duration (mins)	29	15	16	44	12	20
Proportion of time	28%	22%	14%	51%	16%	38%
TELEPHONE CALLS:						
Number of calls	174	133	21	51	22	30
Time on telephone (hours)	19	13	1.2	5.8	1.9	3.2
Average duration (mins)	6	6	3	12	12	20
Proportion of time	9%	6%	3%	15%	4%	9%

Appendix G.1, continued
Comparison with Chronology Record

CATEGORY	STUDY COMPOSITE	MINTZBERG'S COMPOSITE	STUDY RANGE		MINTZBERG'S RANGE	
SCHEDULED MEETINGS:						
Number of meetings	109	105	16	30	14	30
Time in meetings (hours)	103	120	16.5	26.0	10.6	29.8
Average duration (mins)	59	68	44	73	40	98
Proportion of time	48%	59%	33%	56%	38%	75%
UNSCHEDULED MEETINGS:						
No. of Meetings	176	101	20	66	10	55
Time in meetings	30	20	4.3	10.8	1.2	9.6
Average duration	11	12	8	17	6	24
Proportion of time	14%	10%	9%	28%	3%	18%
TOURS:						
Number of tours	42	29	2	26	0	11
Time in tours	3	5	.07	2.4	.2	.5
Average duration	6	11	2	9.5	0	8
Proportion of time	2%	3%	0%	6%	0%	3%
Proportion of activities lasting						
< 9 min	54%	49%	41%	61%	40%	56%
> 60 min	9%	10%	4%	19%	5%	13%

Appendix G.2
Comparison with Contact Record

CATEGORY	STUDY COMPOSITE		MINTZ-BERG'S	
Total verbal contact (hrs)	155		158	
Total number of verbal contacts	501		368	

MEDIA: Percent of contacts/Percent of contact time

Telephone calls	35%	12%	36%	8%
Scheduled meetings (SM)	22%	66%	29%	76%
Unscheduled meetings (UM)	35%	20%	27%	13%
Tours	8%	2%	8%	3%

*PARTICIPANTS: Percent of contact/Percent of contact time

Subordinate	64%	49%	64%	48%
Director (Superior)	5%	8%	6%	7%
Codirector (Peer internal)	11%	16%	5%	5%
Peer external and trade organization	4%	6%	3%	11%
Client	3%	3%	2%	3%
Supplier or vendor	8%	11%	9%	17%
Independent and other	4%	7%	9%	8%

INITIATION: Percent of Contacts

Manager	49%	32%
Opposite party	40%	57%
Mutual	9%	5%
Clock	2%	7%

LOCATION: Percent of Contacts/Percent of Time

Manager's office	53%	33%	75%	39%
Office of subordinate	7%	5%	10%	8%
Office of superior	1%	1%		
Hall or plant	16%	7%	3%	1%
Conference or board room	10%	26%	3%	14%
Away from organization	12%	27%	8%	38%
Peer's office	1%	1%		

Appendix G.2, continued
Comparison with Contact Record

CATEGORY	COMPOSITE		MINTZBERG'S	

PURPOSE OF CONTACT :
  Percent of contacts/ Percent of Contact Time

Nonmanagerial*	2%	1%	0%	2%
Scheduling	13%	5%	15%	3%
Ceremony	5%	5%	6%	12%
External board work	.4%	2%	2%	5%
Total secondary	19%	12%	23%	21%
Status requests and solicita-				
tions	3%	1%	5%	1%
Actions requests	10%	4%	17%	12%
Manager requests	13%	3%	12%	5%
Total requests/solicitations	26%	9%	34%	18%
Observational tours	2%	1%	2%	1%
Receiving information	9%	13%	14%	16%
Giving information	11%	8%	10%	8%
Review	19%	24%	10%	16%
Total informational	42%	45%	36%	40%
Strategy	13%	31%	6%	13%
Negotiation	1%	3%	1%	8%
Total decision making	4%	33%	7%	21%

SIZE OF SM/UM/Tours	SM	UM	Tours	SM	UM	Tours
Percent with 2 people	39%	86%	83%	44%	92%	77%
Percent with 3 people	9%	9%	10%	14%	4%	12%
Percent with 4 people	6%	2%	5%	9%	3%	4%
Percent with more than 4 people	45%	3%	2%	34%	1%	8%

*Tornado safety area

Appendix G.3
Comparison with Input Mail Record

Category	Study	Mintz-berg's	Study Range		Mintzberg's Range	
Number Pieces Received	355	659	35	119	69	172
FORM OF INPUT (%)						
Letter	17%	38%	9%	32%	21%	59%
Memo	46%	16%	24%	61%	3%	25%
Report	17%	25%	13%	22%	12%	32%
Periodical	15%	16%	3%	26%	6%	14%
Clipping	4%	4%	0%	11%	2%	5%
Book	1%	1%	0%	7%	0%	1%
ATTENTION (%)						
Skim	34%	31%	16%	47%	6%	63%
Read	58%	63%	45%	67%	33%	94%
Study	8%	6%	0%	18%	4%	9%
*SENDER (%)						
Sub.	63%	39%	50%	76%	21%	62%
Superior	3%	1%	0%	5%	1%	2%
Peer-ext.	2%	16%	0%	3%	6%	13%
Peer int.	5%		1%	8%		
Trade org.	2%	9%	0%	10%	2%	20%
Client	2%	5%	0%	11%	1%	11%
Supplier	10%	8%	3%	29%	2%	14%
Independent	2%	6%	0%	5%	1%	10%
Publisher	13%	11%	3%	30%	2%	27%
Govt.	1%	5%	0%	5%	2%	12%

Appendix G.3, continued
Comparison with Input Mail Record

CATEGORY	STUDY COM-POSITE	MINTZ-BERG'S COM-POSITE	STUDY RANGE		MINTZ-BERG'S RANGE	
PURPOSE OF INPUT MAIL (%)						
Acknowledgments	1%	5%	0%	3%	2%	7%
Status requests	1%	12%	0%	3%	5%	30%
Solicitations	6%	5%	0%	29%	3%	9%
Authority requests	27%	5%	2%	49%	3%	12%
TOTAL REQUESTS	35%	27%	15%	54%	16%	45%
Reference data	24%	14%	9%	29%	8%	20%
General reports	4%	8%	1%	11%	1%	18%
Periodical news	15%	15%	5%	25%	3%	42%
Events	6%	8%	0%	18%	4%	12%
Reports on operations	9%	18%	0%	13%	8%	30%
Advice on situations	3%	6%	0%	5%	2%	14%
Problems and pressures	2%	2%	0%	8%	1%	4%
Ideas	1%	2%	0%	7%	1%	4%
TOTAL INFORMATION	65%	73%	46%	85%	51%	80%

Appendix G.4
Comparison with Output Mail Record

CATEGORY	Study	Mintz-berg	Study Range		Mintz-berg's Range	
Number of reactions to inputs	35	206	1	12	20	65
Number self-initiated	74	25	3	33	1	15
Total output	109	231	10	45	23	66
Output as a percent of input	31%	35%	8%	74%	16%	62%
Self-initiated as a percent of output	68%	11%	30%	92%	2%	31%

FORM OF OUTPUT MAIL (%)

Letter	23%	47%	0%	83%	30%	56%
Memo	35%	19%	8%	45%	9%	30%
Report	35%	2%	8%	60%	2%	9%
Forwarded letter	4%	18%	0%	10%	8%	30%
Forwarded memo	1%	5%	0%	2%	2%	9%
Forwarded other	3%	9%	0%	20%	4%	18%

TARGET (%)

Subordinate	45%	55%	6%	80%	41%	68%
Superior	18%	2%	5%	39%	2%	6%
Peer external	12%	17%	0%	33%	2%	24%
Peer internal	17%		0%	39%		
Trade organization	3%	5%	0%	11%	0%	12%
Client	1%	7%	0%	2%	3%	22%
Supplier or vendor	2%	3%	0%	10%	4%	8%
Independent	1%	5%	0%	2%	2%	9%
Government	0%	7%	0%	0%	2%	23%

PURPOSE OF OUTPUT MAIL (%)

Acknowledgment input	0%	12%	0%	0%	7%	17%
Reply to written requests	10%	33%	0%	20%	20%	51%
Reply to information received	8%	10%	0%	15%	4%	18%
Forward information to sub.	18%	23%	0%	70%	9%	34%
Forward request to sub.	4%	7%	0%	9%	2%	13%
Write to 3rd party re input	3%	3%	0%	5%	2%	9%
Acknowledge/reply to verbal contact	2%	6%	0%	8%	4%	18%
Write report	28%	2%	8%	45%	2%	9%
Originate letter or memo	26%	3%	5%	67%	1%	8%

Appendix H:

Comparison with Ives and Olson

Appendix H.1
Characteristics of Participating Organizations

	MIS Mgrs.	CIO's
DP Employees (range)	30 - 300	
Information Technology Employees (range)	N/A	84 - 700
other CIO responsibilities*	N/A	
Total for CIO	N/A	108 - 1384
Organizational Level		
Corporate	5	5
Division	1	0
Industry Type		
Manufacturing	3	1
Utility	1	1
Finance	1	
Insurance		1
Service	1	
Government Agency		1
Education		1
Reporting Level (from CEO)		
One	1	1
Two	3	4
Three	2	0

* The manufacturing CIO had responsibility for two IT related product divisions. The government agency CIO had responsibility for the work of 1300 contractor personnel

Source: Ives and Olson (1981, 51)

Appendix H.2
Activities Per Day

ACTIVITY	NUMBER PER DAY (range)					
	CEOs Mintzberg		MIS Mgr. Ives/Olson		CIOs Composite	
Desk work	7	(5 11)	9	(6 17)	5	(2 7)
Phone calls	5	(4 6)	9	(6 14)	7	(4 10)
Scheduled meetings	4	(3 6)	5	(2 10)	4	(3 6)
Unscheduled meetings	4	(2 11)	16	(8 28)	7	(4 13)
Tours	1	(0 2)	2	(0 3)	2	(0 5)
Total activities/day	22		41		25	

	AVERAGE DURATION IN MINS. (range)					
Desk work	15	(12 20)	9	(5 13)	29	(16 44)
Phone calls	6	(5 7)	4	(2 7)	6	(3 12)
Scheduled meetings	68	(40 98)	40	(22 103)	59	(44 73)
Unscheduled meetings	12	(6 24)	5	(4 10)	11	(8 17)
Tours	11	(0 8)	6	(0 11)	6	(2 10)
Average	22		13		22	

	PROPORTION OF TIME					
Desk Work	22%	(16% 38%)	19%	(9% 36%)	28%	(14% 51%)
Phone Calls	6%	(4% 9%)	9%	(6% 14%)	9%	(3% 15%)
Scheduled meetings	59%	(38% 75%)	48%	(30% 67%)	48%	(33% 56%)
Unscheduled meetings	10%	(3% 18%)	20%	(11% 29%)	14%	(9% 28%)
Tours	3%	(0% 3%)	2%	(0% 6%)	2%	(0% 6%)

Source: Ives and Olson (1981, 53)

Appendix H.3
The Nature of Oral Contacts: Comparison with Mintzberg's and CIO study

	MINTZBERG'S COMPOSITE: CEO'S		IVES & OLSON COMPOSITE: MIS MGRS.		STUDY COMPOSITE: CIOs	
MEDIA: % of contacts / % of time						
Telephone calls	36%	8%	31%	13%	35%	12%
Scheduled meetings (SM)	29%	76%	17%	57%	22%	66%
Unscheduled meetings	27%	13%	53%	30%	35%	20%
Tours	8%	3%	not	given	8%	2%
LOCATION: % of contacts/% of time						
Manager's office	75%	39%	69%	58%	53%	33%
Other's office	10%	8%	13%	7%	9%	6%
Hall (or plant)	3%	1%	9%	2%	16%	7%
Conference or board room	3%	14%	8%	26%	10%	26%
Other (Away from organization)	8%	38%	2%	6%	12%	27%
INITIATED BY: % of Total Contacts						
Manager	32%		54%		49%	
Other Party	57%		38%		40%	
Chance (Mutual)	5%		4%		9%	
Clock	7%		4%		2%	

Source: Ives and Olson (1981, 54)

Appendix H.4
Number of Participants in Oral Contacts

Size of Meeting	Scheduled Meetings MIS			Unscheduled Meetings MIS		
	CEOs	Mgrs.	CIOs	CEOs	Mgrs	CIOs
Percent with 2 people	44%	53%	39%	92%	90%	86%
Percent with 3 people	14%	15%	9%	4%	8%	9%
Percent with 4 people	9%	5%	6%	3%	1%	2%
Percent with more than 4 people	34%	27%	45%	1%	1%	3%

Source: Ives and Olson (1981, 54)

Appendix H.5
Types of People With Whom Manager Had Contacts

PERSON:
% of contacts/% of contact time

	CEOs		IS MGRS.		CIOS	
Subordinate	64%	48%	60%	47%	64%	49%
Director (Superior)	6%	7%	4%	7%	5%	8%
Codirector (Peer internal)	5%	5%	not	given	11%	16%
Peer external and trade org.	3%	11%	not	given	4%	6%
Client	2%	3%	not	given	3%	3%
Supplier or vendor	9%	17%	6%	9%	8%	11%
Independent and other	9%	8%	9%	7%	4%	7%
Users	not	given	10%	8%	not	given
Corporate Service Groups	not	given	11%	8%	not	given

Source: Ives and Olson (1981, 55)

Appendix H.6
Primary Purpose of Each Oral Contact

	CEOs		MIS MGRs.		CIOs	
PURPOSE OF CONTACT:	% of contacts / % of contact time					
Nonmanagerial*	0%	2%	not	given	0%	1%
Scheduling	15%	3%	12%	2%	13%	5%
Ceremony	6%	12%	not	given	5%	5%
External board work	2%	5%	not	given	0%	2%
Total secondary	23%	21%	12%	2%	18%	12%
Status requests and	5%	1%	not	given	3%	1%
solicitations	17%	12%	8%	2%	10%	4%
Action requests	12%	5%	15%	5%	13%	3%
Manager requests	34%	18%	23%	7%	26%	9%
Total re- quests/solicitations						
Observational Tours	2%	1%	not	given	2%	1%
Receiving information	14%	16%	24%	18%	9%	13%
Giving information	10%	8%	12%	8%	11%	8%
Review	10%	16%	14%	28%	19%	24%
Total informational	36%	40%	50%	54%	42%	45%
Strategy	6%	13%	4%	21%	13%	31%
Negotiation	1%	8%	not	given	1%	3%
Total decision making	7%	21%	4%	21%	14%	33%

Source: Ives and Olson (1981, 56)

Appendix H.7
Verbal Interaction Analysis by Participant Area: External, Functional, Information Technology (percent of contacts, percent of contact time)

		% Contacts		% time	
PARTICIPANTS	STUDY	RANGE		RANGE	
	COMPOSITE	Min	Max	Min	Max
External	14%	16%	5%	28%	2%	33%
Functional Area	26%	22%	19%	34%	9%	38%
Areas not including IT	40%	38%	32%	56%	25%	53%
Functional &IT	3%	8%	1%	4%	1%	12%
Functional, IT, & external	2%	4%	0%	4%	0%	15%
IT & external	1%	9%	0%	4%	0%	19%
IT & other areas	6%	20%	2%	11%	10%	30%
Areas other than IT	46%	58%	36%	61%	52%	71%
IT only	54%	42%	39%	64%	29%	48%

Verbal Interaction Comparison with Ives and Olson

	% of contacts		% of contact time	
	IS MGRS.	CIOs	IS MGRS	CIOs
Categories Outside of Information Technology Area				
Director (Superior)	4%		7%	
Supplier or vendor	6%		9%	
Independent and other	9%		7%	
Users	10%		8%	
Corporate service group	11%		8%	
Areas other than IT	40%	46%	39%	58%
Categories from Information Technology				
Subordinate (IT)	60%	54%	61%	42%

Source: Ives and Olson (1981, 55)

References

Anderson, Howard. 1989. Using Telecommunications Strategically. *Telecommunications* (January): 41-42.

Barker, Joel. 1985. *Discovering the Future: The Business of Paradigms*. Lake Elmo, Minn.: Infinity Limited. Cited in McNurith (1988a): 13-14.

Benjamin, Robert I., Charles Dickinson, Jr., and John F. Rockart. 1985. Changing Role of the Corporate Information Systems Officer. *MIS Quarterly*, 9(3): 177-188.

Boyle, Robert D. and John J. Burbridge. 1991. Who Needs a CIO? *Information Strategy: The Executive's Journal*, 7(4): 12-18.

Brown, Eric H., Kirk R. Karwan, and John R. Weitzel. 1988. The Chief Information Officer in Smaller Organizations. *Information Management Review*, 4(2): 25-35.

Brumm, Eugenia. 1988a. Chief Information Officers in Service Organizations: A Survey. *Information Management Review*, 3(3): 17-30.

Brumm, Eugenia. 1988b. *Exploratory Study of Chief Information Officers in Fortune Service and Industrial Organizations*. Unpublished doctoral dissertation, University of Illinois at Urbana-Champaign.

Couger, J. Daniel, Robert A. Zawacki, and Edward B. Opperman. 1979. Motivation Levels of MIS Managers versus Those of Their Employees. *MIS Quarterly*, 3(3): 47-56.

Davis, G. B. 1974. *Management Information Systems*. New York: McGraw-Hill, 374. Cited in Benjamin, Dickinson, and Rockart (1985).

Donovan, John. 1989. Interview: From the Back Room to the Boardroom. *Computerworld*, 23(16): 83-84.

Drucker, Peter E. 1988. The Coming of the New Organization. *Harvard Business Review* (January-February): 45-53.

Harris, Catherine L. 1985. Information Power: How Companies Are Using New Technologies to Gain a Competitive Edge. *Business Week* (October 14): 108-114.

Ives, Blake, and Margrethe H. Olson. 1981. Manager or Technician? The Nature of the Information Systems Manager's Job. *MIS Quarterly*, 5(4): 49-63.

Keen, P. 1987. Technology creates simplicity, not complexity. *SIM Network* (April--June): 1-3. Cited in McNurith (1988b): 6.

Kirkley, John. 1988. The Restructuring of MIS: Business Strategies Take Hold. *Computerworld*, 22(12), 79-84: 91-93.

Kolodziej, Stan. 1989. Organizational Impacts of Downsizing: Changes That are More than CPU-Deep. *Computerworld*, 23(26): 71–73.

LaRosa, Patricia Ann. 1985. *Corporate Information Executives: Perceptions Regarding Roles, Responsibilities, and Job Preparation.* Unpublished doctoral dissertation, Arizona State University.

Martinko, Mark J., and William L. Gardner. 1985. Beyond Structured Observation: Methodological Issues and New Directions. *Academy of Management Review*, 10(4): 676–695.

Mason, Florence Margaret. 1984. *The Emergent Information Manager: A Structured Observation Study of the Nature of the Information Manager's Work.* Unpublished Ph.D. dissertation, University of Southern California.

McCall, M. W., Jr., A. M. Morrison, and R. L. Hannon. 1978. *Studies of Managerial Work: Results and Methods.* Technical Report Number 9, Center for Creative Leadership, Greensboro, N.C.

McNurith, Barbara Canning. 1988a. Creating a Vision and Selling It. *I/S Analyzer* (formerly EDP Analyzer), 26(9): 1–12.

McNurith, Barbara Canning. 1988b. Influencing Corporate Policy. *I/S Analyzer* (formerly EDP Analyzer), 26(6): 1–14.

Mintzberg, H. 1968. *The Manager at Work—Determining His Activities, Roles, and Programs by Structured Observation.* Unpublished Ph.D. dissertation, Massachusetts Institute of Technology.

Mintzberg, H. 1973. *The Nature of Managerial Work.* New York: Harper & Row.

Mintzberg, H. 1975. The Manager's Job: Folklore and Fact. *Harvard Business Review*, 5(4): 49-61.

Mintzberg, H. 1990. The Manager's Job: Folklore and Fact. *Harvard Business Review*, 163–176. Reprint of Mintzberg(1975).

Nolan, R. L. 1983. *Managing the Advanced Stages: Key Research Issue.* 75th Anniversary Colloquium papers, Harvard Business School, Cambridge, Mass. Cited in Benjamin, Dickinson, and Rockart (1985).

O'Riordan, P. Declan. 1987. The CIO: MIS Makes Its Move into the Executive Suite. *Journal of Information Systems Management*, 4(3): 54–56.

Perry, Nancy 1986. Managing the IS Power. *HBS Bulletin.* February: 38. Cited in Synnott 1987b.

Porter, Michael. 1985. *Competitive Advantage.* New York: Free Press.

Rifkin, Glenn. 1989. CEO's Give Credit for Today but Expect More Tomorrow. *Computerworld*, 23(16): 75–86.

Sayles, L.R. 1964. *Managerial Behavior: Administration in Complex Organizations.* New York: McGraw-Hill.

Stephens, Charlotte S., Amitava Mitra, William N. Ledbetter, and F. Nelson Ford. The Strategic Planning Process for the Information Executive: Work Characteristics and Implications. *1994 Proceedings of the Southeast Decision Sciences Institute*, Williamsburg, Va.

Stewart, R. 1976. *Contrasts in Management: A Study of the Different Types of Manager's Jobs: Their Demands and Choices.* New York: McGraw-Hill.

Synnott, William R. 1987a. The Emerging Chief Information Officer. *Information Management Review*, 3(1): 21–35.

Synnott, William R. 1987b. *The Information Weapon: Winning Customers and Markets with Technology*. New York: John Wiley & Sons.

Synnott, William R. and William H. Gruber. 1981. *Information Resource Management*. New York: John Wiley & Sons.

Thoreau, Henry David. 1854. *Walden*. New York: Avenel Books.

Toffler, Alvin. 1990. *Powershift*. New York: Bantam Books.

Weick, K. E. 1968. Systematic Observational Methods. In G. Lindzey and E. Aronson (Eds.), *Handbook of Social Psychology* (357–541), Vol. IV, 2nd ed. Reading, Mass: Addison-Wesley.

Index

220   *Index*

About the Author

CHARLOTTE S. STEPHENS is an Associate Professor of Management at the Abbott Turner School of Business at Columbus College. Stephens received her Ph.D. and M.B.A. degrees from Auburn University. She has published over 50 articles, contributed chapters to two textbooks, and presented papers at many national and international conferences. Her research has focused on the role of the CIO.

ISBN 0-89930-920-8

EAN

9 780899 309200

HARDCOVER BAR CODE